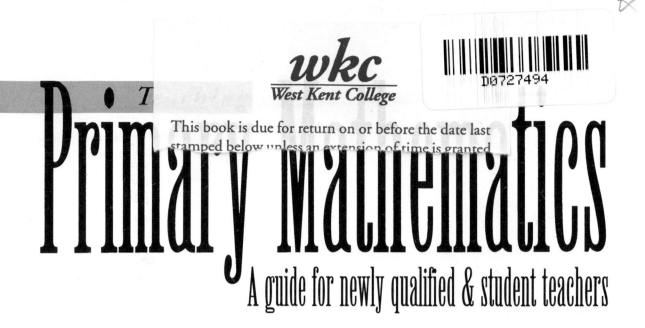

Primary Mathematics

A guide for newly qualified & student teachers

Mike Askew

(with an additional contribution by Michelle Selinger)

Hodder Arnold

A MEMBER OF THE HODDER HEADLINE GROUP

Orders : please contact Bookpoint Ltd, 130 Milton Park, Abingdon, Oxon OX 14 4SB. Telephone : (44) 01235 8227720. Fax : (44) 01235 400454. Lines are open from 9.00–6.00, Monday to Saturday, with a 24 hour message answering service. You can also order through our website at www.hoddereducation.co.uk

British Library Cataloguing in Publication Data
A catalogue record for this title is available from The British Library

ISBN-10: 0 340 63161 9
ISBN-13: 978 0 340 63161 4

First published 1998
Impression number   11   10
Year   2007   2006   2005

Copyright © 1998 Mike Askew

Typeset by Mulltiplex Techniques Ltd.
Printed in Great Britain for Hodder Education, a division of Hodder Headline, 338 Euston Road, London NW1 3BH by Arrowsmith, Bristol.

CONTENTS

ACKNOWLEDGEMENTS

This book attempts to pull together ideas on the effective teaching of mathematics in primary schools, drawing on both research findings and work with teachers. As such, although named author, there are numerous people I would like to acknowledge and thank as they have all, in different ways, contributed to my thinking.

First, my thanks to Michelle Selinger who encouraged me to embark on this book in the first place. Discussion with Michelle on the form and content of the book and her contributions to Chapters 7 and 8 had a great impact on the finished product and doubtless improved it.

Thanks to Margaret Brown, Alison Millet, Tamara Bibby and other colleagues at King's College with whom I have worked on various projects. The long discussions and their emphasis on evidence for what works has been highly influential on my thinking. Outside King's, Sheila Ebbutt, Director of the BEAM Project, must be thanked for her constant friendship, encouragement and enthusiasm.

I would like to be able to acknowledge by name the wonderful teachers who have allowed me access to their classrooms but the list is too long and my memory incomplete. If you happen to be one of those teachers who has had me descend upon your class, I hope you will accept this rather more public thanks for your patience and help.

Writing a book takes its toll on one's personal life. Thanks to Graham Barker for making sure that I did not spend all my time at the word-processor but equally told me when it was time to get on and finish things.

Finally I would like to dedicate this book to Anna and Joshua in the hope that they grow up to enjoy mathematics and take pleasure in using it.

The primary mathematics curriculum

There is currently much concern about national standards in the understanding and use of mathematical ideas and skills. This concern has arisen from the UK's children's comparatively poor performance in international studies and evidence from school inspections.

The solution that is popularly proposed is that a return to 'traditional' teaching methods is required, whatever they may look like. Many people interpret these as more 'whole class teaching', where the teacher is at the front addressing all the children at once. However, this is only one aspect of the primary mathematics curriculum: classroom organisation.

To fully understand the teaching of mathematics in primary classrooms, three aspects of the mathematics curriculum need to be considered:

■ the intended curriculum;

■ the implemented curriculum;

■ the attained curriculum (Robitaille and Dirks, 1982).

The intended curriculum is the curriculum as set out in various documents. The National Curriculum provides, through its programmes of study, a framework for the intended curriculum, but further details are provided through other sources. For example, school text books provide a form of intended curriculum, as do schemes of work prepared by individual teachers or schools. As the name implies, the intended curriculum is the set of expectations or intentions of what children should learn.

The intended curriculum has to be put in place by teachers. Different teachers will set up classrooms and organise their teaching in different ways, and interact with children in a variety of styles. Even with the same intended curriculum, what the children experience may be very different. For example, two teachers may choose to use a text book in very different ways. One may go through each page with the whole class and then set children to work on that page so that the class moves through the scheme at the same pace. Another teacher may set everyone off on page 1 and allow children to work through at their own pace, so that within a few weeks the children are at a range of different points. In other words, the implemented curriculum may be very different from the intended curriculum.

In the end there is the question of what children have learnt. Children differ in their preferred ways of working: some may work best alone, others may benefit more from working as a group. Children also differ in the range of knowledge of mathematics that they come to school with. Some will make more sense of the ideas that they meet than others do. So although a class of children may all experience a very similar implemented curriculum, there will be a range of different understandings for them as individuals. The attained curriculum, what individuals actually learn, is different again.

This book addresses all three aspects of the curriculum. The intended curriculum is explored through looking at the National Curriculum expectations and expanding these to address the key understandings that primary children might develop.

Accounts of classroom lessons, extended case studies of particular activities and suggestions for teaching ideas are used to help develop models for the implemented curriculum.

Findings from research into children's understandings and examples of children's responses to teaching provide some insights into the attained curriculum.

Teaching primary mathematics

A major thread that runs through this book is that teaching mathematics should be based on what research has to tell us about how children learn mathematics and the most effective ways of teaching it. There are no simple 'slogans' that provide the solution to helping children learn mathematics. For example, some authors argue that in teaching primary mathematics you should always 'start with the practical'. However, we now know from research that some children experience difficulties that arise out of too much emphasis on the practical.

The teaching approaches developed here arise out of a wide range of research findings. Although diverse, there are three recurrent themes that do inform the activities discussed here:

■ the importance of mental strategies;

■ the links between problem solving and mathematical understanding;

■ the importance of careful assessment of what children can do.

THE IMPORTANCE OF MENTAL STRATEGIES

For many years it has been the accepted wisdom in teaching primary mathematics that starting with practical activities is best. However, research is beginning to show that for some children this can lead to them seeing mathematics as a practical activity. Rather than using physical objects to develop mental ideas, these children continue to rely on the physical object to do the mathematics. For example, rather than commit to memory the number bonds to 10 (pairs of numbers that add to 10), children, often secretly, continue to rely on their fingers.

Throughout the book are examples from research of difficulties children have in making the link between the practical and the mental, and suggestions for ways in which they might be helped to do this.

THE LINKS BETWEEN PROBLEM SOLVING AND MATHEMATICAL UNDERSTANDING

Another theme that emerges from research is that there are close links between understanding an idea and being able to apply it in a problem solving situation. Again, popular wisdom on teaching suggests that children need to learn 'the basics' before they can apply them to problems.

The approach taken here is much more one of using problems to engage children's interest, to challenge them to think about mathematics and to provide the motivation to learn new ideas.

THE IMPORTANCE OF CAREFUL ASSESSMENT OF WHAT CHILDREN CAN DO

A great deal of research draws attention to the diversity of ideas about mathematics that children develop. Many of these ideas do not closely match the accepted mathematical understanding.

It is also clear from research that simply 'telling' children the correct idea is not the most effective way of challenging the alternative understandings that children have. Assessing children's understanding is not simply to do with checking that they can get correct answers. It requires dialogue between teachers and children about the methods used, so that misunderstanding can be made explicit and addressed.

In the chapters that follow, many examples of children's understandings are provided to illuminate some of the ideas that you may encounter in classrooms and to reinforce the importance of this ongoing diagnostic assessment.

Effective teaching

The Effective Teachers of Numeracy Project (Askew, Brown, Rhodes, Wiliam and Johnson, 1997) identified a group of teachers described as connectionist in their approach to teaching primary mathematics. These teachers emphasised connections in the sense of:

■ valuing children's methods and explanations;

■ sharing their own strategies for doing mathematics;

■ establishing connections within the mathematics curriculum, for example linking fractions and decimals.

These connectionist teachers were identified as 'highly effective' teachers of numeracy as the children in their classes had, during a year, achieved a higher average gain on a test of numeracy in comparison with other classes from the same year group.

The importance of discussion

Central to all the activities that you will find here is the role of discussion in helping children develop mathematical ideas: discussion between teacher and children, discussion between children. It is our belief that learning mathematics is essentially a social process and comes about through the sharing of ideas. It follows from this that the most important resource in the classroom is you, the teacher. The teacher is in a position to introduce new mathematical ideas, direct children's' attention to the mathematical aspects of activities, to encourage children to share their understandings with each other.

For these reasons you will find that most of the activities here need to be set up through discussion – it would be very difficult to turn them into workcards! While this does place organisational demands on you, ways in which this can be made manageable include:

■ talking through activities with the whole class – children who are not about to do an activity will need less instruction when their turn does come;

- getting children who have already done an activity to explain it to others;

- using reporting back sessions at the end of lessons to set up work for later lessons;

- 'timetabling' yourself to have a particular time with each group when you can focus on discussion.

Challenge and enjoyment

Often people talk about the need to make mathematics 'fun'. In order to do this activities are 'dressed up' as games or put into contrived contexts. Some teachers also think it is a mark of good teaching if the children have not realised that they are doing mathematics.

Rather than mathematics being fun, it needs to be enjoyable and for most children being challenged is enjoyable. The mathematics here is not disguised or made to seem 'fun'. Mathematics should be enjoyable but pleasure can arise out of meeting a challenge and reaching a satisfactory conclusion. I hope you and your children find some such enjoyment from the ideas presented here.

2

WHAT ARE WE TRYING TO ACHIEVE WITH CHILDREN IN NUMBER?

Introduction

One way of thinking about the teaching of number in primary schools is to consider it as made up of three strands:

- **computation:** arithmetical calculation and procedures;

- **process:** the application of number to problems;

- **conceptual:** understanding the relationships between different mathematical ideas (Thompson, 1994).

Traditionally the first of these three, computation, has been treated separately from the other two. Many people still equate primary school mathematics mainly with computation, and particularly with the aim of children leaving primary school well versed in the four rules of arithmetic. This usually means concentrating on paper and pencil methods and regarding the ability to do long division as the pinnacle of achievement. Children are expected to learn computational techniques and methods first and only later learn to understand and apply them, if at all.

However, recent studies, both of children's learning and teaching practices in other countries, suggest that separating out the teaching of computation from both the process and conceptual aspects may not be the best approach. In particular more attention needs to be given to pupils' processes and strategies in carrying out arithmetic.

In this chapter I look at some broad themes in the teaching of number in primary schools that encourage the links between computation, process and concepts. These themes are developed into teaching activities in Chapters 3 through 6, shown as Activity Boxes and Activity Banks.

A framework for basic number sense?

In a well-argued article, McIntosh, Reys and Reys (1992) suggest that there are three strands to children developing good number sense:

- knowledge of and facility with numbers;

- knowledge of and facility with operations;

- applying knowledge of and facility with numbers and operations to computational settings.

Each of these three strands has a number of parts.

Knowledge of and facility with numbers involves developing:

- an understanding of ordering of numbers;

- being able to represent numbers in a variety of forms;

- having a sense of both the relative size of numbers (that 1 000 is 100 times larger than 10) and the absolute size of numbers (what a 1 000 bricks might look like in comparison to 10);

- building up a system of benchmarks – mental images that help give a sense of number sizes (for example knowing that 250g is about the same as a packet of butter).

Knowledge of and facility with operations includes understanding:

- the effect of operations (for example, knowing that there are two aspects to division, repeated grouping and sharing – see Chapter 4);

- the mathematical properties of operations (for example the commutative nature of both addition and multiplication – see Chapter 3);

- the relationship between operations (for example, that finding the difference between two numbers can either be done as a subtraction or by adding on).

Applying knowledge of and facility with numbers and operations to computational settings includes being:

- able to identify the appropriate operation to use in a problem;

- aware that there may be several different strategies that would work;

- inclined to find and use an efficient method;

- inclined to check over results to make sure they are sensible.

National Curriculum expectations

The National Curriculum programmes of study at both Key Stages 1 and 2 emphasise the importance of children developing methods of working and computing with number that are both flexible and effective. This includes being able to work mentally and explain methods orally. Recording of methods should be varied and include records that relate to mental work. There is also the expectation that children should be able to use calculation methods with understanding.

Children are also expected to have access to and to use a variety of practical resources and contexts to explore number structure. In Key Stage 1 children are expected to encounter numbers greater than 1 000. Any equipment should be used accurately and appropriately.

The National Curriculum also expects children to have access to and experience of electronic means of calculating. This includes using calculators not only as a tool for calculating with realistic data but also to explore number. They also need to use computer software, including a database.

Teaching and learning about flexible and effective methods of calculating

The history of teaching mathematics in school is peppered with different 'solutions' and advice on how best to teach number. At one time there was support for the idea that children could be left largely to their own devices and to discover mathematics for themselves. Teachers were only there to encourage or facilitate these discoveries, but not to teach directly. At the other extreme were teaching approaches which concentrated on drilling children in particular methods and routines, regardless of whether the children understood what was going on. Understanding, it was argued, would follow later.

However, it is becoming clear that there are no simple answers to the question 'how can I best teach number?' Children respond differently to experiences and what works for one child may not work for another. Some children do seem capable of 'discovering' mathematics for themselves (although often this is because they have learnt some ideas at home), while others need more direct instruction. As indicated in Chapter 1, what is required is a 'connectionist' approach where children and teachers work together on developing mathematical understandings.

In order to help children become confident in number they need to have broad and balanced experiences. Broad in the sense of encountering mathematical ideas through a variety of practical resources and contexts. Balanced in the sense of any particular way of working not being dominant. For example, if children only ever work with numbers through paper and pencil methods then that is not providing them with this breadth and balance.

To help achieve this breadth and balance there are at least six sorts of resources and contexts that children need to experience:

- mental mathematics;
- lines, cards and grids;
- electronic means of calculating;
- practical materials;
- realistic problem contexts;
- paper and pencil methods.

For more details on each of these see Askew, Briscoe, Ebbutt *et al* (1995) and Askew, Briscoe and Ebbutt *et al* (1996).

Mental mathematics

Ultimately mathematics is a mental activity. While practical work can help children develop mental images, practical work on its own is not sufficient. Young children can be asked to show you how they know something, using blocks or their fingers. Getting them to give a verbal explanation is more difficult but is an essential step in 'going mental'. Teachers are sometimes sceptical that very young children can work in this way. Indeed when you first ask 'what was in your head' young children will often respond with 'nothing'.

This difficulty that young children have in explaining is sometimes interpreted as young children not having any mental images. But at any age, being asked to explain what is going on inside your head is difficult. If you have never been asked before it can take time before it is clear what is being expected. Such responses may be less to do with children's inability to reflect on their own thinking processes and more to do with not previously been asked to reflect on what is in their heads or knowing what an acceptable answer might be.

Research is beginning to show that by expecting children, from an early age, to reflect on how they worked something out, to picture things in their heads and to manipulate mental objects helps young children begin to develop mental facility.

This does not mean that practical experiences have no role in early mathematics. With young children the activity may need to be set up with physical equipment, as this can hold and direct their attention and provide a means of checking answers. However, it needs to lead to an element of 'in the head', otherwise young children may be left with the impression that mathematics is all about practical work.

Two ways to help children begin to articulate their mental processes are:

- providing model explanations, either through you explaining your own methods or through hearing more experienced children explain;

- asking children to 'pretend' that something was happening in their heads and asking them to explain that.

Under the cloth, while a simple activity to set up, requires the children to hold information in their heads and has an elements of challenge and prediction, all of which contribute to their mental ability.

Under the cloth

A teacher was playing 'under the cloth' with some reception children in the first term of school. A number of counters were put out and everyone in the group counted to make sure they knew how many were there. These were covered with a cloth and again everyone was asked how many were there. The teacher lifted the cloth to check with the children that the number was unchanged (important as some children seemed to think that the teacher was about to perform a conjuring trick!). The teacher removed some counters from under the cloth and asked the children how many they thought were left.

Once children had begun to get confident with the activity then they were asked to explain how they knew the answer. This required some patience and perseverance to get beyond the 'I just know' response.

Five counters under the cloth, the teacher took out two.

Harriet:	It's three, three.
Teacher:	Gosh, you sound sure, how do you know?
Harriet:	I know, it's three.
Teacher:	How do you know?
Harriet:	I do.
Teacher:	Can you try and tell me how you know it's three?
Harriet:	You took out one, then you took out four, that's three.

[Try reading Harriet's response with the interpretation that by 'four' she meant 'the fourth'.]

Four counters under the cloth, two removed.

Sam:	Two.
Teacher	Why is it two?
Sam:	It just is.
Teacher:	How do you know it's two?
Sam:	It has to be.
Teacher:	Yes, but how do you know it has to be?
Sam:	There are two (pointing to the two removed) so there has to be two.
Teacher:	Why will there be two?
Sam:	There were four and two and two are four.

Once they had the idea the children went on to take it in turns to put out an initial number of counters, count them, remove some and challenge each other to say how many were left.

Lines, cards and grids

Becoming confident with number involves having a repertoire of symbolic images to draw upon. Number lines, number grids of various types (hundred squares, multiplication and addition squares and so on) and number cards can provide sources of rich activities together with a range of symbolic images that can support the development of mental images and strategies. For example, on a 0 – 99 hundred square the effect of adding 10 can be explored with young children and they can see that counting on ten separate units has the same effect as 'dropping' down immediately one space on the hundred square. Thus they become able to instantly add on 10.

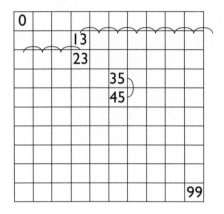

Place value cards can be used to help children understand how numbers are composed of separate sets of hundreds, tens and ones.

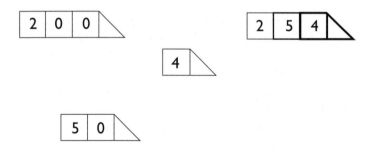

Similarly number lines, as in Chapters 3 and 4, can be powerful tools in helping children understand the number structure and develop mental calculation strategies.

Electronic methods of calculating

It seems to be a popular myth that calculators de-skill children and remove the need to think about the mathematics. However, research evidence increasingly demonstrates that free access to calculators at all stages of schooling does not lead to any lowering of standards. In fact the reverse appears to be the case: free access to calculators can lead to improved attainment.

PrIME

The PrIME project (Primary Initiative in Mathematics Education) was a nationally funded curriculum development project in primary mathematics in English and Welsh schools from 1985 to 1989. As part of the project, some schools provided children with free access to calculators from the age of five.

One local education authority gave a written test to 116 eight year-olds who had been involved in the project and had had free access to calculators for either four or seven terms. The performance of these children on the test was compared with 116 other children chosen at random from the non-project children in the authority. Before giving it to the children, the test was carefully revised by teachers so that it would not give advantage to children who either did or did not habitually use calculators.

There were 36 test items and on 28 of these, the project children got a higher percentage correct. On 11 of these items, the project children scored at least 10% more and on one item the success rate of the project children was 30% higher. On the eight items where the non-project children scored as well or higher, they only out-performed the project children by a maximum of 5.3% (Shuard, Walsh, Goddwin and Worcester, 1991).

Calculators serve two distinct but complementary purposes in the classroom:

■ as a teaching and learning aid through which children can explore numbers;

■ as a tool for handling realistic data.

CALCULATORS AS A TEACHING AND LEARNING AID

Calculators can provide young children with access to the way that numbers are represented in a dynamic form. Well-planned calculator activities challenge children and can encourage them to predict what will happen next. For example, even on very simple calculators it is easy to set up a constant function, for example to repeatedly add 2 (usually done by keying in 2 + + = = = ...).

By setting up the constant function of adding 1, the calculator can be made to 'count' by repeatedly pressing the equals key. Young children who can count out loud can explore this by counting and simultaneously pressing the key. This requires the development of the skill of co-ordinating the two actions of pressing the key and saying the number word. It also helps children understand the link between the spoken and symbolic representation of number. Finally, it can help children extend their counting skill by the pattern of numbers that the calculator presents. In all of these areas, watching how the children interact with the calculator provides valuable assessment information.

Dividing by four

Fielker (1985) discusses examples of activities where the calculator is used to stimulate mathematical activity. One such example involved getting children to explore the results of dividing by 4.

Asked to find the answer to 18 ÷ 4 most of the children could explain the answer of 8.5 as .5 being five-tenths or a half.

By looking at the results of dividing 16, 17, 18 and 19 by 4, the children were challenged to find out what they could about numbers which gave an answer ending in .25 when divided by 4.

The children were able to come up with generalisations like:

If the number you have ends in 5 you always get .75 or .25.

Elizabeth could take this one step further, noticing that if the digit before the 5 was even, then the answer ended in .25, and it ended in .75 if the digit before the 5 was odd.

Jason was able to deduce that

To get .75 in an answer you will have to divide a number which is 1 less than a number which 4 goes directly into.

He was then able to go on to produce similar statements about .25 and .5.

CALCULATORS AS A TOOL FOR HANDLING REALISTIC DATA

Problem solving activities in classrooms have often had to be contrived and presented with simple figures so that the children could cope with the calculations. Rather than helping children appreciate the practical role that mathematics can serve, this can lead to them seeing mathematics as something peculiar to school. Children often have an awareness of the cost of items in the shops and have difficulty reconciling this with the unrealistic costs presented in text books. As the children do not appreciate that the figures have been simplified in order that they can do the calculations, they come to see 'school mathematics problems' as not being related to real life.

Make up a story

Asking children to invent stories to go with calculations can reveal a great deal about the children's thinking.

McIntosh (1978) gave children the calculation 43 – 27 =. After the children had worked out the answer, he asked them to make up a story to go with the calculation. The following are stories he got from children who could do the calculation correctly.

My dad is 43 and my mum is 27. How old is my sister?

My friend and I went out to play. We started off at his house which is 43, went to my house at 27 and ended up at number 16.

One teacher tried this with her Year 5 class, asking them to make up stories to go with 5 ÷ 2. One child wrote:

Video tapes cost £2 each. I had £5 to spend and bought 2 and a half tapes.

Having calculators available enables children to concentrate on the problem solving aspects of realistic problems, rather than the calculational part. Thus realistic data can be worked with and children gain a better understanding of the application of mathematics.

Similarly, using computers for calculating can release children from having to focus their attention on finding answers. The speed of computers means that children can rapidly produce many examples using, for example, a spreadsheet. This allows the children to concentrate on observing patterns and making hypotheses and generalisations.

Both calculators and computers encourage children to be accurate and express themselves clearly. Unlike humans, the machine cannot interpret the meaning of unclear instructions.

Practical materials

There are two sorts of practical materials that children need to work with to help develop their understanding of number. 'Structured' materials are commercially produced objects usually specifically designed to embody a particular mathematical idea. For example, base 10 blocks are structured to demonstrate the structure of place value: there are single 'unit' cubes, sticks 10 units long, 10 by 10 squares equivalent to 100 units and cubes with a volume of 1 000 units.

Children also benefit from working with unstructured materials – everyday objects that can be used for counting and measuring (for example, bottle tops, buttons, pebbles, lengths of ribbon, leaves).

Two plus two

Research by Hughes (1986) demonstrated that from an early age children can operate with small numbers when they are linked to objects (for example knowing that two elephants and two more elephants makes four elephants). But they find it difficult spontaneously to put into a context numbers presented in an abstract form.

For example, one way of working out the answer to '2+2' is to reinterpret this as 'two elephants and two more elephants'. The sort of the conversations Hughes had with children is typified by Patrick's (four years 1 month) responses (pages 47–8):

MH:	*How many is two and one more?*
Patrick:	*Four.*
MH:	*Well, how many is two lollipops and one more?*
Patrick:	*Three.*
MH:	*Well, how many is two elephants and one more?*
Patrick:	*Three.*
MH:	*Well, how many is two giraffes and one more?*
Patrick:	*Three.*
MH:	*So how many is two and one more?*
Patrick:	*Six.*

Furthermore, there is little evidence to suggest that facility in putting ideas into context gets easier as children get older.

Practical work is not at all useful if the children fail to abstract the mental mathematics from the experience. Research is confirming what experienced teachers know: that this process of abstraction is far from easy.

Rule of thirds

The Children's Mathematical Frameworks project (Hart *et al.* 1989) demonstrated that the link between practical work and understanding the formal mathematics is shaky for many children.

Groups of six children of different levels of attainment were individually interviewed on four occasions:

- prior to a topic being taught;
- immediately before the move from the practical to the more formal aspects of the topic (for example, going from using base 10 blocks to find the answer to a subtraction calculation to a paper and pencil method);
- immediately after the introduction of the formal aspects;
- again three months later.

Across several topic areas (subtraction, fractions, areas, volumes, equations and ratio), amongst children from age eight to thirteen, a consistent 'pattern of thirds' emerged:

Approximately one-third of the pupils had some access to the formal mathematics even before the teaching began, one-third did not acquire the formal aspects, and the remaining third learnt the formal aspect with varying degrees of success.

For the children who already had some understanding of the formal mathematics before the teaching, the time spent on practical work, from which they were expected to abstract the ideas, was probably unnecessary.

Even the third of children who demonstrated some degree of success had difficulties. Probing in subsequent interviews revealed that there were still some misunderstandings which prevented short-term success from developing into longer term understanding – for example, believing that the striking out of figures when subtracting by decomposition resulted in the total number changing.

Similarly, a detailed study and analysis of a group of pupils learning place value from tens and units blocks indicated that the blocks themselves served only as a vehicle for teacher talk. The learning came about from the way the teacher talked about and handled the blocks, rather than through the pupils' own discoveries (Walkerdine, 1988).

The main message from such research is that while practical work can be useful, it needs to be chosen carefully, and accompanied by careful discussion with children to establish the extent of their understanding. Children's success on a practical task should not be taken as an indication of understanding of the abstract. The ways in which children perceive links between the practical and the abstract need to be the subject of considerable discussion between children and teachers.

Realistic problem contexts

It is becoming clear that being able to apply knowledge of number is not distinct from developing understanding. Solving 'realistic' numerical problems has been demonstrated as an effective way of helping children appreciate the need for mathematical ideas. Chapter 6 explores the role of realistic problems in detail.

One particular set of realistic problems that are worth mentioning here are those that involve measuring. The need to develop and use increasingly accurate measuring tools provides a good way into developing the number system. For example, needing an answer that is more accurate than 'between 1 and 2 cm' can be used to introduce fractions and decimals.

Paper and pencil

The main advantage of paper and pencil is that it extends our 'mental screens', our mental screens being the internal images and impressions of mathematics that we all carry around in our heads even if we are not always aware of them. Such images may be auditory as well as visual: one person adding 36 and 42 mentally may silently talk through adding 6 and 2 and 30 and 40, another may see the figures while another may just 'know' that the answer is 78.

Keeping several ideas in the head at once is difficult and paper and pencil helps us 'hold onto' ideas. But paper and pencil does not provide an alternative to mental mathematics; mental activity is still important. Paper and pencil methods are not ends in themselves but means to an end. The process of calculation should lead to insight, not numbers.

It is important that children become aware both of their own strategies and those that others use. Explaining out loud is one way of recording, as is using paper and pencil to show their own methods. This requires a shift in teacher expectations. Asking children to find the answer to 76 – 38 can either be treated as

- **an exercise** – expecting children reproduce a standard method that they have been previously taught or as

- **a problem** – challenging children to try and find a solution, knowing that they have not been taught a method of solution.

The advantage of the latter is that it both provides assessment information for the teacher and acts as a base from which methods can be developed and refined. This is taken up in Chapter 5.

Paper and pencil has one advantage over working things out mentally, in that a permanent record is provided.

Summary

I suggest that effective teaching of number needs to pay attention to:

Concepts, processes and calculations
These three are related aspects of understanding and each helps support and develop the other.

The importance of mental methods
Children need to have plenty of opportunity to explain their mental processes and to hear the methods that others use.

The importance of children's explanations
Encouraging children to explain how they arrived at correct answers as well as incorrect ones provides valuable insights into their mathematical thinking.

Providing different representations of numbers
A range of models of the number system, including diagrams, measures, number line, grids and cards as well as symbols, practical materials and electronic means of calculating.

Treating calculations as problems
Expecting children to make sense of numbers and calculations and interpret them in a meaningful way rather than simply trying to 'spot' which method to apply.

Using 'realistic' contexts
These help children both appreciate the application of number and provide a foundation for the introduction of new ideas.

Chapters 3 through 6 develop these ideas in more detail.

3

DEVELOPING CHILDREN'S UNDERSTANDING OF THE NUMBER SYSTEM

Introduction

Probably the most important aspect of the primary number curriculum is children's understanding of our number system.

A good understanding of place value is one key aspect of familiarity with the number system. But understanding the number system is not only to do with place value. Children also need experiences which will help them understand how the desire by mathematicians to solve calculations like 3 – 7 leads to the invention of negative numbers.

Similarly, the need to find answers to calculations like 3 ÷ 4 is part of the origin of fractions. Coming back to place value, fractions can be linked to decimal fractions and both can be linked to percentages and ratios.

Understanding the number system requires children to build up a rich set of interconnections between place value, fractions, decimals, ratios, percentages and negative numbers. This means that teaching needs to provide activities that focus on the links between these aspects of mathematics rather than treating them as separate topics.

For children to be confident and fluent in the number system they need to have:

■ secure understanding of place value;

■ understanding of the relationships between numbers, for example knowing that 2 001 is greater than 1991 or that 3 000 is ten times smaller than 30 000;

■ understanding of the relationships between different representations, for example knowing that ¾, 0.75 or 75% are all equivalent but might be used in different contexts.

This chapter looks at these links, why they are important, some of the difficulties children have in understanding the links and suggests teaching strategies that might help children develop better understanding.

Concept mapping

How do you understand the links between

place value   **fractions**   **decimals**

ratios   **percentages**   **negative numbers**

One way to explore understanding of the links is to make a concept map.

On a piece of paper arrange the above terms in a way that you think reflects the way the terms relate to each other.

Draw single-or double-headed arrows linking pairs of terms and write on the shaft of the arrow a description of the nature of the link. For example:

percentage ⟶ decimal
can be expressed as

It is helpful to do this with a colleague and compare the different links identified.

Children's concept maps are a powerful device both for helping teachers identify what children know and helping children become aware of what they already know and alerting them to areas to work on.

For example, a teacher of a Year 5 class at the beginning of a unit of work on fractions got the children in groups to produce posters of everything they knew about fractions, including the sort of calculations they could do. The groups presented their posters to the rest of the class and by listening the teacher was able to identify two or three aspects of fractions that she and the class needed to work on.

A teacher of Year 2 children gave pairs of children a photocopied sheet with a picture of a calculator in the centre and several statements around the outside about what a calculator can do, for example, 'you can add on a calculator' or 'you can show 9876543210 on the calculator display'. The teacher read out the statements and the pairs of children had to decide whether they thought it was possible. If they decided the calculator could do what was claimed, they drew a green arrow to the statement, if they thought it was impossible, a red arrow and a yellow arrow if they were not sure. The teacher was surprised that only one pair realised that 9876543210 was too long to fit on the calculator display and nobody thought that the calculator could be used to double numbers.

The original idea of concept mapping comes from Novak and Gowin (1984).

National Curriculum expectations

At Key Stage 1 the expectations for understanding the number system as set out in the programmes of study indicate that children need to become confident in counting, initially up to 10 and that they should be able to use their ability to count to find out the number of objects in a collection and be able to check the total. Children should also be able to count in steps, for example in steps of 2 from 10, recognise odd and even numbers and build on this to recognise other sequences, for example 3, 6, 9, 12 ...

They need to develop the skills of reading, writing and ordering numbers eventually up to 1 000 and understand the place value aspect of the digits in a number, for example knowing that the 3 in 736 is actually representing 30. They should also begin to round numbers to the nearest 10 or 100.

Key Stage 1 children are expected to work with simple fractions, decimals and negative numbers in contexts, for example half of the children in the class, recording money using decimal notation, extending the number line to include negative numbers.

These ideas are built up in the programme of study for Key Stage 2 so that children have the skills of reading, writing, ordering and rounding numbers and understanding the place value aspect of the digits for numbers beyond 1 000. In addition they are expected to be able to multiply and divide by powers of 10 when there are whole-number answers.

Their understanding of fractions, decimals and negative numbers needs to be extended to include decimals in the context of measurement and to be able to use fractions and percentages to estimate, describe and compare proportions of a whole.

Teaching and learning about the number system

TEACHING AND LEARNING ABOUT COUNTING

To adults, being able to count seems to be a simple process – learn the number names in order and attach them to objects. But for the child learning to count requires the co-ordination of several aspects.

Counting

Gelman and Gallistel (1986) have identified several components of learning to count including:

The stable order principle
This means appreciating that number names need to be recited in the same order each time.

The one to one principle
When children have grasped this principle they realise that one number name needs to be linked to one object.

The cardinal-ordinal link
When counting a collection of objects the child initially has to link number names to individual items but the final number announced not only applies to the last item (the ordinal or ordering aspect of counting) but also then gives the total number of items in the set (the cardinal or quantifying aspect of counting). So in counting a collection of, say, five objects, the announcing of five when pointing to the last object simultaneously declares that there are five objects in the set. Adults tend to mark this transition by a rising intonation in their voice when numbering the last object. Children who do not appreciate this, when asked, 'so how many are there', will count all the objects again!

That any object in a collection can be counted first
If children are asked to count a collection of objects laid out in a row, but asked to start with, say, the third object (indicated by pointing to it and asking them to count the objects but start with that particular one) then children who do not appreciate that the starting object is immaterial may either say they cannot count the objects or count 'one, one, two, three' and so on, going back and pointing to the first object on the second count of one.

The work of Gelman and Gallistel suggests that children need plenty of experience of working with objects that they can move around, rather than printed collections to count. Teachers can explicitly model the actions of counting by touching and moving objects aside. Careful observation of and listening to children's strategies when they count the objects can reveal which of the counting principles they have achieved and with which they need more help.

The use of a 'silly' puppet is also a valuable assessment tool. The teacher, through the puppet, makes mistakes in counting a collection. Can the children identify the errors the puppet is making?

Number rhymes are also important. Children do need to memorise the list of number names to ten and then twenty. As these are a fairly random collection of sounds, there is no avoiding the rote learning of them. The social nature of sharing rhymes can at least make this pleasurable.

In recent years research attention has begun to focus on the understanding of number that young children bring to school. This represents a shift towards examining what young children *can* do rather than what they cannot do.

Just saying the words

Munn (1994), researching the knowledge of mathematics that young children bring to school, notes that it takes time for children to realise that counting actually provides information about a collection rather than simply being something 'you just do'.

Before beginning formal schooling, many young children can:

■ count meaningfully;

■ use terms like 'more' and 'less' appropriately;

■ have some understanding of addition and subtraction with small numbers;

■ invent strategies for solving problems.

While children can display such competencies, it is also apparent that their understandings of the purposes behind skills like counting do not always accord with how adults perceive the task. One child was surprised to be asked what counting is used for and replied 'But counting's just saying the words!'

While 'learning the words' is clearly important, it is only a part of what is involved in learning to count. For example, when asked for a specific number of bricks, some children who can recite the number sequence quite adequately will simply grab a quantity of bricks. A major task of the teacher is to help children come to a view of counting as a purposeful activity.

There is something of a tradition in early years mathematics that children should be exposed to numbers gently, starting with numbers to five, then ten, twenty and so on. It is now becoming clear that the way children come to understand the number system is much more like learning to talk – there is no neat structure. In language children are not restricted to short words before they are introduced to longer ones – many young children soon learn to say 'television'.

Looking at the numbers that children encounter in their everyday lives makes it clear that they do not simply meet small numbers. House numbers, telephone numbers, older sister's scores on computer games and so on all present children with a variety of number sizes. The skilful teacher acknowledges this range and works with it rather than ignoring it.

Split the beans

A reception teacher was working with a group on splitting five beans: each child had a piece of paper with two circles drawn on it and five dried beans. The children in the group took it in turns to put some beans in each circle, checking each time that there were still five in total and discussing if their way of splitting them was different from the ways already on the table.

The children were then challenged to count out their favourite number of beans, to split them between the two circles in lots of different ways and use another piece of paper to record what they had done.

Sandy announced that 30 was her favourite number, accurately counted out that number of beans and proceeded to record as pairs of numbers 15 different splits. As her teacher remarked 'I was surprised. I have done this activity before but always asked the children to do it with, say, six beans. Giving them the choice of which numbers revealed so much more about what they can do.'

The way our number system works and the names that we use for numbers, means it ironically gets easier with bigger numbers! Children have particular difficulty with the 'teens', due to the idiosyncratic number names and the similarities with the multiples of 10 (for example '13' and '30'). Once the structure of the 'teens' has been learned, young children's verbal counting ability increases rapidly to 29 or 39, indicating a development of their understanding of the 'decade' system. Contrary to popular belief, it is not easier to work with numbers to 10, then 20 then 30 and so on, as it is only with the larger numbers that the naming system becomes clear: six-ty, seven-ty, eight-ty, nin(e)-ty. Life would be a lot easier if we counted one-ty-one, two-ty-four rather than 11 and 24.

That's a hard one

A Year 2 teacher had her class working in pairs. Each pair was given a selection of number cards and asked to pick out two that they liked. These two were to be the first two numbers in a number sequence pattern and the children had to continue the pattern. By selecting number cards of different values the teacher was able to match the activity to different levels of attainment.

Billy and Joe had chosen 79 and 99 from their cards. When the teacher joined them the boys had written down 79 99 119 139 159. Asked to explain how they had worked it out, it became clear that all the calculations had been done by counting on 20 on their fingers. Their teacher decided to work on adding on 10 with the boys. Asked what was 10 more than 55, both boys started counting on their fingers.

Teacher: *No, let's work on a quicker way. Sit on your hands!*

Along with the boys, the teacher sat on her hands and asked what 10 more than 50 was. Eventually the boys came up with 60. Following this with 10 more than 70 and 60, the boys came to see that the pattern in the names helps and it was a very short step to be able to add 10 to 45, 78 and so on.

But when their teacher asked them what 10 more than 16 was, both boys went back to counting on their fingers! It struck the teacher that the language was not going to help in this case and she quickly drew a diagram of a stick of 10 and 6 ones. By playing around with this the boys accepted that it would be 26, and after a couple more examples the teacher felt they had cracked it. As she got up to move, she asked: 'So what's 10 more than 12?' 'Oh, that's a hard one again,' groaned Billy.

The general consensus from the research is that young children need to have more experience of larger numbers. Calculating with large numbers is not suggested but the National Curriculum does specify that Key Stage 1 children should gain experience of numbers to 1 000. This may help them develop a better understanding of the number system. Restricting young children to numbers under 20 may be doing them a disservice because, as indicated above, up to around 30 the naming of numbers does not mirror the place value system.

TEACHING AND LEARNING ABOUT PLACE VALUE

A good understanding of place value is one key aspect of familiarity with the number system. If children understand place value then:

- they can develop mental calculation methods that are effective and efficient;

- paper and pencil methods of calculation can be carried out with understanding;

- multiplying and dividing by 10 or multiples of 10 becomes simple;

- decimal fractions and percentages can be understood as extensions of the place value system rather than new topics.

Sometimes children's understanding of place value is limited to being able to identify how many tens there are in, say, 372, but as I point out below there is rather more to understanding place value than this.

To develop children's understanding and confidence, some of the core understanding required at earlier and later stages of primary school are set out below.

Early place value understandings

Children need to be able to:

- count in ones, forwards and backwards from any number up to 100, leading to being able to count in twos, fives and tens forwards and backwards from any number up to 100 and use their counting skills to efficiently find out totals, for example, counting in fives to find out how much a bag of 5p coins is worth;

- read numbers presented in a variety of forms, for example reading numbers off a 1–10 number track or 0–10 number line

leading to 0–100 number line and number lines where only some of the numbers are marked, for example identifying the number that the arrow is pointing at in each of the lines below

and also working with number squares, both 0–99 and 1–100 to read and locate numbers;

- read any number up to 1 000 (not simply reading the digits);

- know the number complements to 10, that is, given any single digit you can tell what needs to be added to it to make 10;

- add 10 to a single digit, without having to count on 10 single ones;

- add and subtract 10 to any two-digit number;

- know the importance of the order of the digits, for example, given two cards each with a single digit on can make two different two-digit numbers, read each one and say which is the larger.

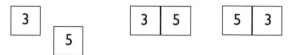

Later place value understandings

Children need to be able to:

- use knowledge of place value to 'disaggregate' numbers in a variety of ways, for example knowing that 57 can be expressed as 50 + 7 or 40 + 17 or 60 — 3;

- add or subtract a multiple of 10 to any two-digit number without counting on;

- quickly find the complement of a two-digit number to 100, that is, what needs to be added to the number to make 100;

- read any number and appreciate the pattern of grouping the digits in threes: that 34578641 needs to be grouped in threes from the right – 34 578 641 – and then read from the left, using knowledge of hundreds, tens and ones for each grouping: thirty-four *million*, five hundred and seventy-eight *thousand*, six hundred and forty-one;

- multiply mentally by 10, 100, 1 000 leading to division by 10, 100;

- use decimals, fractions and percentages to represent the same amount in different ways, for example can express 0.125 as a fraction and percentage.

Pre-requisites for learning place value

Work by Ronshausen (1978) suggests that before being introduced to place value, a child needs to be able to flexibly count from 0 to 9 which includes being able to:

- identify a set given the number

   — for example select a set of say four objects from a collection of different sized sets when asked to pick out the set of four

- create a set given the number

   — for example when asked to put out six objects can do so

- correctly name the number of objects in a set

   — for example shown a collection of, say, eight objects can say there are eight

- can do all of the above but presented with numbers in a written form rather than spoken, and can record as number symbols sets of 0 to 9 objects

- can count from 1 through 10 both with and without objects.

Place value is based on three principles:

- the idea of treating a group of objects as a 'unit';

- using the same symbols repeatedly;

- using the position of a digit to indicate the size of grouping it represents.

Together these three principles make the place value system of recording numbers both economical (no matter how big a number I want to record no new symbols need inventing) and efficient. While this economy and efficiency make place value mathematically powerful, it also accounts for why some children find difficulty in fully understanding it.

The idea of treating a group of objects as a 'unit'

This is the core idea upon which place value is built – the idea that a 'unit' might be a group of things, rather than a single item.

For the Key Stage 1 child, the unit is a single whole entity. When children count collections of objects, each object is treated separately as a single object. This treating of the objects individually is, as indicated above, a key skill in learning to count.

But as children's learning about addition and subtraction grows, so they have to progress from the use of 'unit' to refer to a single object to the use of 'unit' to refer to a group. For example, in learning the complements to 10, if children are going to commit to memory that the complement of 7 to 10 is 3, then it is helpful to think of the 7 as a group, a unit that has 7 members, rather than thinking of it as seven separate items. Similarly the 3 has to be thought of as a unit, so the 'triple' of 7, 3, 10 is a triple of three different 'units'.

Being able to move flexibly between different 'units' would seem to be a key aspect in learning efficient mental strategies. In adding 10 and 8 children can find the answer in different ways. Some may need to create 10 separate units (ones), using fingers, practical equipment or tally marks, and then a further 8 ones to count the entire collection to find the answer.

Children who have begun to be able to work with groups as units will be able to develop more efficient methods. For example, one child may be able to treat the '10' as a unit in itself, to start counting on 8 from, ten, eleven, twelve, and so on until they reach the answer of 18. Another child may be able to treat the '10' as a 'unit' to add to a second 'unit' of 8 and know rapidly that the answer is 18.

Tallying

While some Key Stage 1 children are able to work with flexible units, research suggests that many children still work with 'units' that are always single items, even at the end of Key Stage 2.

Askew, Bibby and Brown (1997) give the example of a nine-year-old who was working out what to add to 278 to get 500. Although the boy could do addition and subtraction of hundreds, tens and units when the calculation was set out in a vertical form, he found the answer to this calculation by counting on from 278 to 500 by making separate tally marks and then going back and counting each of the tallies. Amazingly he got the correct answer of 222.

When asked about the pages of vertical calculations in his exercise book, it was clear that the boy was only dealing with single digits in each column. So to find the answer to

$$358$$
$$+\ 237$$

the boy treated it as three separate additions of single digits and did not 'read' the numbers as 'three hundred and fifty-eight' and 'two hundred and thirty-seven'. He also had to use his fingers still to carry out the additions. So although on paper it looked as though he was competent in dealing with hundreds, tens and units, in reality the boy had not progressed very far from adding single digit numbers (and was not even doing that very efficiently).

Moving between different units is not simply something that children have to be able to do to deal effectively with understanding place value. To understand multiplication a shift in the 'unit' is needed from single units to units that are groups of numbers. One understanding of the meaning of 9 multiplied by 5 requires the '9' to be treated as a single composite unit to be taken five times.

The introduction of fractions and decimals marks another change in the use of units. In Key Stage 1 and the early years of Key Stage 2 units consist of whole numbers, either single 'ones' or composite units (a 'ten'). However, a shift into regarding units as parts of a whole (one half, one tenth) also has to be dealt with.

Grouping as units

On a sunny afternoon a reception teacher took her class into the playground.

She told the children that for that afternoon, five was to be a 'forbidden' word. She chalked four small circles on the ground, one fewer than the forbidden word, and four larger circles.

The class chose a nonsense name for the forbidden word, plonk. As a group they counted together one at a time, placing one pebble in each small circle. When the four small circles were full, the fifth pebble, created a 'plonk' and all five pebbles were put into one of the larger circles. The next pebble went into one of the now empty small circles and the teacher and children discussed what it should be counted as. They agreed to call it plonk-one.

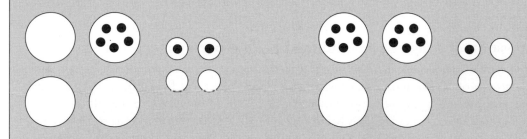

'plonk-two'   'two plonk-one'

The count continued: one, two, three, four, plonk, plonk-one, plonk-two, plonk-three, plonk-four, two plonk, two plonk-one and so on until four-plonk-four was reached.

The teacher stopped and asked the children what they thought the next number would be after plonk-four and two-plonk-four.

Later on they repeated the activity but this time six was the forbidden word and a different nonsense name chosen.

Using the same symbols repeatedly

The practice of successive grouping means that only ten symbols – 0 to 9 – are needed to record the number of groups of any magnitude: three groups of ones, eight groups of tens, five groups of millions.

Naming of parts

Research evidence shows that Japanese pupils develop an understanding of place value from a younger age, and this appears to be a result of the way number names are explicitly spelt out (twenty-two as the equivalent of two-tens two) (See Stigler et al, 1990.)

This explicit naming of the place value does not begin to appear until the hundreds: three hundred and twenty nine. In dealing only with numbers up to 100 at the same time that they are learning to write, some children learn that there is a one-to-one correspondence between the words spoken and what is written. Thus twenty-two requires two symbols: 22. Unfortunately this rule does not apply in the hundreds and leads some children to record incorrectly. For example, three hundred and twenty-two becomes written as 30022.

Using the position of a digit to indicate the size of grouping it represents

Using the same symbols repeatedly means being able to distinguish between whether using a 2 and a 4 represents two groups of 10 and four ones or whether the digits represent four groups of 10 and two ones. It is conventional in our number system that placing a digit immediately to the left of another indicates that a grouping ten times bigger is being represented. This convention leads to the need for zero to mark places where there is no grouping. Two hundred and four could be recorded 2 (space) 4 but would 3 6 be three hundred and six or thirty-six written sloppily?

A Year 1 class explored this by working on filling in a 0–99 hundred square 'reading' off blank spaces by knowing the tens are at the front of the row and the units at the top of the column. At the same time they wrote underneath on the board the number as an addition of tens and ones and pairs of pupils modelled it, in hoops by putting out cubes.

The class got into discussion on what the next number would be (agreed 100) and where to place it on the grid – split between in the same row as the 99 or at the start of the next column. Teacher extended the grid and asked what would go in the space for 103. There was much discussion about where to put the extra hoop, and how to record it (why wasn't it 13, 31 or 1003?).

Understanding of place value in secondary school

Evidence from research in secondary schools suggests that many pupils leave primary school with a shaky understanding of place value. The Concepts in Secondary Mathematics and Science (CSMS) research found that only 42% of 12-year-olds and 57% of 15-year-olds could correctly write in figures 'Four hundred thousand and seventy three'. Even having been told on the test paper that in 5214 the 2 stands for 2 HUNDREDS, asked what the 2 stands for in 521 400, only 22% of 12-year-olds and 43% of 15-year-olds answered correctly (Hart, 1981).

Assessments by the Assessment of Performance Unit (APU) further suggest that by eleven whole number place value presents difficulties for some children. A large sample of eleven-year-olds were asked to put the correct number in the box:

$572 = (5 \times 100) + (7 \times \Box) + (2 \times 1)$.

Only 52% correctly answered 10 as the missing number (Assessment of Performance Unit, 1991).

Developing flexibility with place value

Since the English naming structure for whole numbers does not explicitly spell out the place value structure for numbers under 100, one popular teaching approach is to use practical 'models' of the number system. These models emphasise this 'unit' ten structure: base 10 blocks with sticks of 'tens' that can be handled as a single unit, hundred squares that are 10 unit squares wide.

It may be that this emphasis on being able to say that there are seven tens in 73 may help in speedy written vertical calculations. However, the introduction of vertical recording of additions and subtractions of two-digit numbers before children can effectively carry out these calculations mentally may hinder the development of mental strategies as well as lead to misunderstandings and mistakes (Fuson, 1992).

Understanding the structure of whole numbers may be better developed by working with children on being able to partition numbers in a variety of ways. For example, being able to treat 73 as 70 and 3, or 60 and 13, or 80 less 7 or 2 less than 75 may provide not only a better understanding of number structure but also help pupils develop effective mental strategies.

Over-reliance on the use of base 10 materials possibly encourages the idea that the only acceptable way to partition a number is into whole tens and ones. Use of number lines where every 'one' is marked may encourage the use of single units (ones) beyond the point at which they might be useful and inhibit the growth of ability to select and use a range of 'units'.

One approach that appears to have potential in both helping pupils understand whole number place value and help develop mental strategies is the use of an empty number line (Beishuizen, 1995). For example, to add 36 and 22 the model looks something like:

I am starting at 36 and first I am going to add on 20

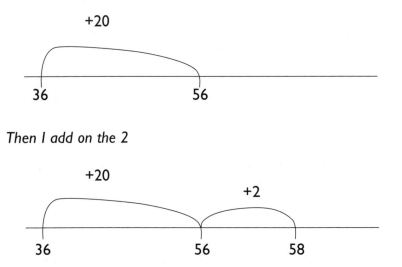

Then I add on the 2

So, 36 add 22 is 58

(Note that in using a blank number line, questions of scale are not considered – the + 2 jump is not in proportion to the + 20 jump, but that is not important.)

Place value is conventional

Just as there is no 'natural' reason that green should be the colour that allows drivers to proceed at traffic lights, so there is no 'natural' reason for us to use place value to record numbers. Each is a convention, making life simpler (and safer) if everyone abides by the rules of traffic lights and place value.

However, as adults used to dealing with numbers expressed in the form of place value, it is easy to see place value as a property of numbers or collections of objects, rather than a convention. Walkerdine (1988) in her research explored how teachers presented activities to children which, in the teachers' terms, enabled the children to 'discover' place value. Through careful analysis of classroom dialogue Walkerdine suggests that rather than discovering place value through handling tens and units blocks, it was the way the teacher talked about and handled the blocks that enabled the children to appreciate the conventions of place value.

Teaching and learning about negative numbers

Many teachers were surprised to find that the National Curriculum expects children in Key Stage 1 to become familiar with negative numbers. How could young children be expected to learn some mathematics which could not easily be demonstrated with practical experiences or that they could not see? But if children can talk about witches, unicorns, creatures from out of space as if they 'really' existed, why not negative numbers?

Children working with calculators will quickly discover that some of the 'rules' of arithmetic that they have come to understand appear to be broken when using a calculator. For example, children know that if there are six cubes on the table, then it is impossible to subtract eight. However, the calculator will do this, providing a way into discussing the idea of negative numbers.

PrIME

The PrIME project (Primary Initiative in Mathematics Education) was an important nationally funded curriculum development project in primary mathematics in English and Welsh schools from 1985 to 1989.

One strand looked specifically at the impact calculators might have on children's learning of mathematics if children had a calculator each and were allowed to use them in the same way that adults do: whenever they wished to. Starting with classes of six-year-olds the project looked at the ideas that children encountered and what they learned.

One feature noted by the project was the early age that children encountered negative numbers through experimenting with the calculator and trying out 'impossible calculations' like $7 - 8 =$. A book about this part of the project (Shuard, Walsh, Goddwin and Worcester, 1991) gives lots of examples of ways in which the children encountered negative numbers and how they came to be able to happily work with them.

For example, Jenny was playing a subtraction game: starting with 50 in tens and units blocks, she and her partner were taking it in turns to roll a dice and subtract that amount. When Jenny was down to 3 and rolled a 5 she said 'I can't take it away. I would owe two.' When she tried this on the calculator she read the display as 'take away two'. This led her to try and make other negative numbers which she could do. The teacher posed her the challenge: 'If the answer is −1, what is the question?' Jenny produced a pattern of questions:

$1 - 2$

$2 - 3$

$3 - 4$

and so on. She knew that the answer to what needed to be taken away from 100 to give −1 was 'easy … one hundred and one'.

Children can also be helped to develop the idea of negative numbers by playing 'imaginary box' activities. Ask the children to imagine you have a box. Now ask them to imagine that you put three cubes in the box. Ask them to imagine you put in another five cubes. How many in the box now? What happens if you now take out six cubes? Activities like this can be extended to discuss situations like an imaginary box with five cubes in it. What happens if you take out 7 cubes?

Experience of working with number lines also helps children develop the idea of extending numbers back beyond zero. For example, one teacher working with her class of six-and seven-year-olds was playing 'back to zero'. The children were asked to start with ten, do something to it to make it bigger and then in exactly two steps say how they would get back to zero and what the intermediate values were. The children told the teacher the steps and she recorded them as they went along, both as a string of calculations and as hops on a number line. Typically, they said things like: 'ten, add ten, that's twenty, subtract five, that's fifteen, subtract fifteen that's zero'. The teacher recorded something like:

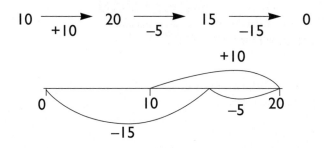

One girl opened up a whole new range of possibilities when she said: 'ten add five that's fifteen, subtract twenty that's minus five, add five that's zero'.

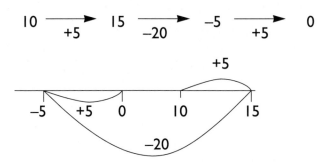

Teaching and learning about fractions, decimal fractions and percentages

Many children (and some adults) fail to fully understand the links between fractions, decimal fractions and percentages because they were taught as three separate topics in school.

Learning to interpret fractions and percentages is as important, if not more so, than simply being able to do the calculations. Using simple contexts can help children grapple with issues of interpretation, further develop their facility in manipulating the figures and reveal to the teacher aspects to work on.

Pie charts

A teacher gave his Year 6 class the following information.

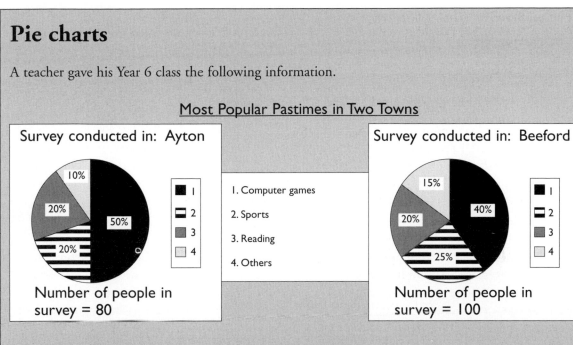

Most Popular Pastimes in Two Towns

The children were asked to make two statements about the popularity of computer games in each town. While everyone wrote that computer games were the most popular in each town, many children went on to argue that computer games were equally popular in each town, because the same number of people had chosen them.

Interestingly, asked to compare the number of people who had chosen reading, many children said it was the same in each case, as both were 20%.

The teacher learned a lot about the children's ability to interpret information and the need to distinguish between samples and total populations. The variety of responses from the children made for a rich class discussion and helped the teacher plan subsequent work.

To work effectively with decimal numbers, children need to extend their understanding of place value with whole numbers. This is not altogether simple. As Swan (1990) points out, there are many situations in everyday life where a dot separates two different units: time, 3.45 pm, or the number of overs left in a cricket match, 6.2. The idea that decimals are an extension of whole number place value and not some new type of number separated by the dot is clearly an idea that is not easy.

Another challenge that learning decimals presents to children is in distinguishing between the concepts underpinning whole numbers that extend to the decimal system and those that do not. For example, the use of zero acts as a place holder in both whole numbers and decimals, but the placing of zero on the right hand end of a number with or without a decimal part has very different effects. Adding a zero to the end of 25 has a very different effect to adding a zero to the end of 2.5. This is one reason why the 'short-cut' of adding a zero to multiply by ten is not helpful in the long-run to children – the rule breaks down when you multiply a decimal.

Similarly, pupils learn that with whole numbers the more digits the larger the number but this generalisation does not extend into decimals: 2 000 is larger than any three digit number, but 0.1256 is not larger than 0.2.

Understanding of decimal place value

Wearne and Hiebert (1988) identify three stages in developing understanding of decimal place value.

First, children have to be able to read meaning into the symbols.

To understand 5.46 $\times$ 3.8 = , meaning must be brought to 5.46 and 3.8 in the form of some models for the numbers: a diagram, thinking of the numbers in terms of measures (5.46 m) or having a sense of their position on the number line. Appropriate meaning also has to be brought to '$\times$' and '=', interpreting them in the context of decimals. This is not straightforward as, for example, interpreting '$\times$' as 'groups of' may present difficulties in understanding what 3.78 'groups of' means. A better meaning for multiplication in this context is the area model — finding the area of a rectangle 5.46 units by 3.8 units makes more sense.

Second, children need to be able to link the steps in a calculation with the underlying concepts.

For example, appreciating that the calculation 5.46 $\times$ 3.8 = includes the multiplication of hundredths by tenths which will result in thousandths and so the answer must have three decimal places. Any rule for the placing of the decimal point can then be linked to this conceptual understanding.

Third, children need to be able to interpret an answer sensibly.

So for 5.46 $\times$ 3.8 = this would mean appreciating that the answer must lie between 15 and 24.

Misunderstanding of decimal place value

Assessment of 150 000 pupils aged 11 or 15 by the Assessment of Performance Unit (APU) found two common errors in children's understanding of decimals: the 'Decimal Point Ignored' (DPI error) and the 'Largest is Smallest' (LS error).

The DPI error is a result of children choosing largest or Smallest numbers on the basis of them being interpreted as whole numbers rather than decimals. Thus in ordering 0.07, 0.23, 0.1 from smallest to largest children working with the DPI misconception treated the numbers as 7, 23, 1 and gave an answer of 0.1, 0.07, 0.23. In fact 31% of eleven-year-olds assessed did give this answer.

One issue arising from the DPI misconception is that pupils can arrive at the correct answer by incorrect reasoning. Choosing 0.625 as the **largest** number out of 0.625, 0.25, 0.375, 0.125, 0.5 is the correct answer but it is also the answer that would be arrived at through reasoning with the DPI error.

The LS error is related to children thinking that the size of a decimal is related to the number of decimal places: the more decimal places a number has, the smaller it is, regardless of the digits involved. So 0.475 would be regarded as smaller than 0.33. Since a correct generalisation for whole number is that the more digits the larger the number (a whole number with three digits is always larger than a two digit number, irrespective of the digits), it might seem that the LS error partly arises out of some viewing of the decimal point as providing 'symmetry' to a number.

A further aspect to the LS error demonstrated by pupils was that when numbers being compared have the same number of decimal places, the 'largest' is chosen as the 'smallest'. Hence 0.625 is selected as smaller than 0.125.

These findings have implications for both the teaching and assessment of decimal fractions. The National Curriculum PoS for Key Stage 2 includes the introduction of decimals to two places in the context of money and measurement. The everyday use of referring to £1.25 as 'one pound twenty-five' may, for some pupils, encourage the development of the DPI error.

As discussed earlier, the issue here is one of making clear to pupils what 'unit' is being worked with. In everyday usage 'one pound twenty-five' conflates two units – the pound explicitly and the penny implicitly. The two, if seen as representing any 'unit' is seen as representing two 'tens' rather than two 'tenths' and the decimal point is simply something separating the pounds from the pence. In using money as a model for decimal notation, pupils need to be made aware of the pound as the unit and the digits after the decimal point as referring to fractions of that unit.

ACTIVITY 1   *Put it in place*

This is a game to help children develop their understanding of place value. It requires children to be working at a symbolic level so they will need to have had experience of activities involving grouping and exchanging before playing the game. In developing strategies for winning the game, children have to reason things through, so making links with using and applying mathematics.

Organisation

Children will be working in pairs. Each pair will need a set of 0 to 9 number cards and each child needs a simple board to lay the cards out on and paper and pencil to record their numbers and scores.

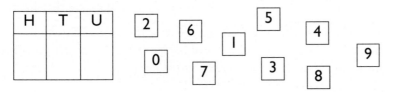

Starting off

Shuffle the cards and place them face down. Turn the top card over and explain to the children that they can place it in any one of the three columns to represent that number of hundreds, tens or ones.

The game continues by children taking it in turns to look at the top card and deciding which column on the board to place it in. The winner of each round is the player with the larger number. The players should record the number that each created, together with who scored a point for that round.

Each round starts with the cards being replaced, shuffled and placed face down again.

Developing the activity

Leave the children to play ten rounds of the game.

Sharing outcomes

Discuss with the children the strategies they developed to decide where to place the cards.

A key insight from the game is that for some rounds the winner is clear before all the places have been filled. For example, drawing a nine and placing it in the tens column cannot be beaten. Do the children appreciate this?

Questions to ask

■ How many will this three represent if I place it in this column?

■ If I hope to make the largest number, which column do you think it is best to place this two in?

■ Which numbers are easiest to decide where to place?

■ If you draw a six how do you decide where to place it?

ACTIVITY 1   *Put it in place (Continued)*

Providing for differentiation

The basic structure of the activity is simple enough for children to engage with it, even if their understanding of place value is not very good. The activity can be made simpler by restricting it to tens and ones.

Assessment opportunities

- Can the children accurately read the numbers that they recorded?

- Can they tell you approximately how much bigger one number of a pair is than the other?

- Can they explain to other children strategies they have developed for playing the game well?

Progression

- Rather than having to place each card on their own playing board, children can place a card either on their own board or their partner's.

- Put a decimal point on the board.

- Each player's score at the end of a round is calculated as the difference between the two numbers.

Consolidation

- Play the game but the aim in each round is to create the smallest number.

- Make a set of 'target' cards, for example, biggest even number, nearest to 500, a multiple of three and so on (encourage the children to make up their own targets and add them to the set) – a target card is turned over before each round.

- Play a calculator version of the game: when a card is turned over the player announces what value it is to have and adds it on a calculator. For example in round 1 a player draws a 4 and decides it will be four tens so she enters 40 into her calculator. On the next round she draws an 8 and decides that this will be hundreds so she adds 800 to the 40.

- Play the game using a 0–9 die or spinner instead of cards.

- Ask the children to select three cards from 0–9. How many different three-digit numbers can they make? Can they put them in order? What about numbers with up to three digits? What if you can use a digit more than once?

- How many different numbers can be made with two cards, three, four and so on. Is there a pattern and rule?

Links within the mathematics curriculum

- Developing strategies for playing the game encourages reasoning and logic (Using and Applying).

- Realising how many different numbers can be made from three different digits is part of algebraic thinking.

- Generating their own two-or three-digit numbers, children can use these for practising addition or subtraction.

ACTIVITY 2 *Percentage race*

This activity should help children to develop mental facility in calculating simple percentages. As it requires them to share strategies for calculating percentages and examine which are most efficient, it has links with using and applying mathematics.

Organisation

You need to prepare a pair of dice, one marked 5%, 10%, 10%, 15%, 20%, 25% and the other marked 20, 40, 60, 80, 100, 120. Each pair of children will also need to make a die similar to the one marked in percentages. Each child will need a copy of an activity sheet with three rectangles, each divided into small squares and containing 20, 40 and 60 squares.

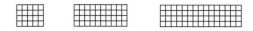

Starting off

Work with the children on how to find 10% of an amount. Remind them about mentally multiplying and dividing by 10. To find 10% of 50 some children may divide by 10, while others may say 'what do you have to multiply by 10 to get 50?' Discuss with the children this link between multiplication and division.

Roll the number die and announce the number rolled. Ask the children to work out 10% of that amount and to jot their answer down on paper. Do not take answers at that point but after four or five rolls, ask them to find the total of their answers and discuss those.

Invite a child to roll both dice. Ask the children to mentally find the answer. For example, 15% of 40.

Invite individuals to come to the front and explain how they found the answer.
Repeat for four or five further rolls of the dice.

Developing the activity

Give out the activity sheet. In groups of six, ask the children to work in pairs and for each pair to work with a different grid: the 20, 40 or 60 grid.

Roll the percentage die and ask the pairs to shade in that percentage of their grid.

After three rolls of the die, stop and set the groups off to discuss the following:
Whose grid will be shaded in first if we carry on rolling the die?

Sharing outcomes

Get pairs of children to come to the OHP or board and argue their case.

After you have heard the different ideas, go back to rolling the die and pairs shading. This time continue until the whole grid has been shaded. Provided the children have calculated the percentages correctly, they should have all completed their grids at the same time.

Discuss why they all finished together.

Questions to ask

- Who expected that the smallest grid would be filled first. Why was it not?

- What would happen if we included a grid of 10 squares?

- Would the game be fair if we included a grid of 10 squares?

ACTIVITY 2 *Percentage race (Continued)*

Providing for differentiation

This is an activity that is designed to work at different levels. At the basic level it is about helping children to develop mental facility in calculating simple percentages. At a more sophisticated level it introduces the idea that percentages allow comparisons of ratios and challenges misunderstandings that children might have about the size of a percentage and the amount of which a percentage is being found.

Assessment opportunities

The children are likely to be split between:

■ those who think the pairs with the 40 grid will finish first, because there are fewer squares to shade;

■ those who think the pairs with the 60 grid will finish first, because there are more squares to get shaded each time;

■ those who realise that because it is a percentage that is being shaded, that the size of the grid does not matter.

As you go round, listen out for these three perspectives and note which children you will invite to present their case.

Progression

Give out the percentage die to each group. In sixes, pairs each choose a different grid. Pairs take it in turns to roll the die and shade in that percentage on their grid.

Is this a fair game? Children who are not sure will need to play the game a few more times until they have sufficient results to look at what is happening.

Consolidation

Children play 'collect 100'. In pairs they need the percentage die and an ordinary die. They take it in turns to roll the pairs of dice, treating the number on the ordinary die as tens, so a roll of 3 is 'read' as 30. Each player works out the percentage of this amount as given by the other die. So a roll of 15% and 4 means finding 15% of 40, i.e. 6. That player jots that amount down. On the next turn they add the amount calculated to that already collected, that is, they keep a running total. The winner is the first player to reach or cross 100.

Links within the mathematics curriculum

Prepare a die with a mixture of fractions, decimals and percentages: 5%, 0.1, $\frac{1}{10}$ 15%, 0.2, $\frac{1}{4}$. Challenge the children to play the above games with this die.

Links across the curriculum

Get the children to look out for examples of the uses of percentages in newspapers and magazines, cut out and collect them and make them into a poster.

ACTIVITY BANK FOR THE TEACHING ABOUT THE NUMBER SYSTEM

Activities about counting

Calculator count

Set up a constant function on the calculator to get it to count in 1s (on calculators without a constant function key, this is usually achieved by clearing the calculator and pressing 1 + + =. Repeated pressing of the = key results in the repeated addition of 1.

Which has more?

Give each child two small bags containing a different number of a collection of small items, for example buttons. Choose numbers that you think are 'on the edge' of children's understanding. For example, one child might have 8 and 10 objects, while another might have 18 and 21. Challenge the children to find out which bag has more in it and to use paper and pencil to show how they found out.

Fill the circles

Prepare a photocopy of a sheet for each child with about a dozen empty circles on it. Each circle should be large enough for children to easily write a single-digit number in it. Children take it in turns to roll a 'spot' die and record in numeral form the result in one of their circles. When pairs have filled up all the circles they swap sheets. They take it in turns to roll the die again, this time crossing out the numbers.

Activities about ordering numbers

Using number lines

Introduce the children to a variety of number lines:

the number track

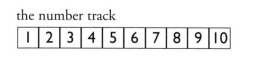

the 0–10 number line – numbers marked

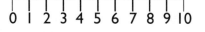

the 0–10 number line – no numbers, just unit divisions

ACTIVITY BANK FOR THE TEACHING ABOUT THE NUMBER SYSTEM (Continued)

the 0–10 number line – no markings, just 0 and 10

the 0–100 number line – all numbers marked

Extend each of these versions of the number line to 0–30 and 0–100.
Use them to get children to play various games, for example:

Put them in order: provide children with some number cards appropriate to the level that they are working at. For example, children working on a 0–30 number line would be given around a dozen numbers less than 30. Children take it in turns to turn over the top card and mark where it is on the number line.

Three in a row: Children can use any of the numbers 0–5 if working to 10, 0–15 if working to 30 and 0–20 if working to 100. They take it in turns to choose any two numbers (they can use the same one twice if they wish) and combine them using addition and subtraction (and multiplication and division if working to 100). Can they get three in a row on the number line without their partner squeezing a number in between?

Show me where

Work with the children on making a number line and slide: fold a piece of thin card or stiff paper to make a long channel, with the back edge higher than the front. Mark an empty number line on the top of the front edge.

In a different colour make an arrow marker that sits inside the channel and can be moved along to point at different parts of the number line.

Ask the children to imagine different end points for the number line and then to position the arrow to show various numbers. For example, beginning at zero and ending at 20, can they show where they think 15 would be marked? Discuss how they decided where to put the arrow.

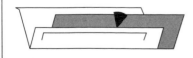

Activities about place value

Grouping in tens

Provide children with opportunities for putting collections of objects into groups of ten. Examples include: bundling straws into tens and ones; putting counters or dried beans into bags or small containers with ten in each; joining interlocking cubes into tens and ones; threading beads onto strings in sets of ten. Talking about 'tens' and 'singles' or 'ones'.
Encourage children to arrange the materials with 'ones' to the right of 'tens'.

Exchanging activities

These build on and extend grouping activities by using different objects to represent either a one or a ten.

- Play place value bingo. Groups need a place value baseboard each, a pool of base 10 materials, sets of 0–9 cards and a die. Children take it in turns to roll the die and take that number of 'ones'. When ten ones have been collected, these are exchanged for a 'ten'. The children put their tens and ones on the place value board with the 'ones' to the right of the 'tens'. They then place digit cards underneath the objects to record the total. The winner is the first person to reach an agreed total, say fifty.

- Play place value bingo but using objects to represent 'tens' which are not ten times bigger but distinguishable from the 'ones' by agreement. For example, red counters for tens, yellow for ones. As with the base ten materials children arrange these on the place value boards with the 'tens' to the right.

- Play place value bingo where the objects representing 'tens' are identical to those representing 'ones' and are only agreed to be representing tens by virtue of their position on the board.

The Gattegno grid

Put a grid like this on the board or overhead projector.

100	200	300	400	500	600	700	800	900
10	20	30	40	50	60	70	80	90
1	2	3	4	5	6	7	8	9

Work with the children on reading off by tapping a number in each row and dealing with the lack of match between number of words and digits (three hundred and forty seven (4/5 words) 347 (3 digits)).

By adding extra rows this can be extended upwards into thousands and ten thousands, or downwards into decimals.
(The board named after the influential mathematics educator, Caleb Gattegno. To read about his work see Brown et al, 1989).

ACTIVITY BANK FOR THE TEACHING ABOUT THE NUMBER SYSTEM (Continued)

Activities about negative numbers

Back and forward

Provide children (or get them to make) a number line from −20 through 0 to 20. Pairs of children will need two dice: one ordinary die and one marked with + on three sides and − on the other three. Starting with their counters on zero, they take it in turns to roll both dice and add or subtract accordingly. So a counter on 3 would move to −2 if the child rolled a − and 5. Can either player reach 20 or −20?

The answer is

How many questions can the children think up where the answer is −1? What about −10? −100?

Activities about fractions, decimal fractions and percentages

Shade it in

Children work in pairs, a sheet of A4 paper is folded to create 16 regions. Each pair will need a die marked ½, ¼, ⅛, ⅜, ¹⁄₁₆, blank. The children take it in turns to roll the die and shade in that fraction on the paper. They should write the fraction, in words (a quarter) and symbols (¼). Agree a scoring system with them, one that includes bonus points for being able to name a shaded fraction in more than one way (this is ¼ so it is also two-eighths and four-sixteenths).

Fraction dominoes

By placing a domino with one set of dots above the other it can be used to represent two different fractions.

How many different dominoes can the children find that are equivalent to ½, ¼, ⅛ etc.?

Here is a correct domino fraction calculation:

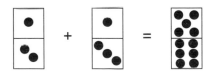

Can the children make up others? Can they make up some using four dominoes?

ACTIVITY BANK FOR THE TEACHING ABOUT THE NUMBER SYSTEM (Continued)

Equivalences

Draw a chart like this on the board:

Fraction % decimal

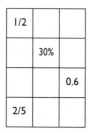

1/2		
	30%	
		0.6
2/5		

Children have to fill in the blanks.

Get them to make up one of their own to swap with a friend.

Squeeze

In pairs, children have a calculator and number line marked 0 at one end and 1 at the other. They take in turns to choose two numbers from 1 to 19 and make a fraction, which they mark on the number line. The winner is the first person to have marked three fractions in a row without their partner 'squeezing' one in between them. Encourage the children to use a calculator to convert their fraction into a decimal fraction to make it easier to decide where to place it on the line.

Number line equivalences

Use the empty number line to explore the differences/similarities in fractions/percentages/decimals. Explore with the children the distinction between marking the point and marking off the distance.

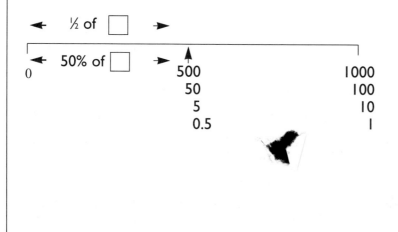

4

DEVELOPING MENTAL METHODS OF COMPUTATION

Introduction

- I have £2 001 pounds in a savings account. How much will be left after I have paid £1 999 for a motor-cycle?

- The current electricity bill shows a meter reading of 3 642 units. The previous reading was 2 978 units. How many units have been used this quarter?

How would you work out the answer to these two problems? Most people are more than happy to work out the answer to the motor-cycle problem in their heads. But the second problem is not quite so straightforward. You may have felt you wanted to set it out as a 'formal' subtraction calculation. Even if you felt happy working it out in your head, jotting down some intermediate steps in the calculation might be necessary.

Both of these problems are essentially subtractions – to work each one out on a calculator you would enter the first number, hit the subtraction button and enter the second number. However, finding the answer without using a calculator does not mean that a subtraction is necessarily carried out: knowing that you need to add 2 to 1999 to make 2001 is a popular method. Writing down

$$2001$$
$$- \underline{1999}$$

and 'doing a take-away', starting with trying to subtract 9 from 1 (remember being told to always start with the units?) might eventually lead to the right answer but is more time consuming and more likely to involve a slip-up.

In carrying out a calculation, two questions have to be asked of the chosen method:

- **Is it effective** – do I feel confident that the method I have chosen will give me a correct answer?

- **Is it efficient** – do I feel confident that the method I have chosen will get me the correct answer with minimum effort?

Asking yourself 'what do I need to add to 1 999 to get 2 001?' is, for most people, the most effective and efficient method. The decision over which method to use is less clear cut in finding the difference between 3 642 and 2 978. Some people are confident in working out mentally what to add to 2 978 to make it up to 3 642, others feel more confident finding the answer using a paper and pencil method.

Dealing with calculations flexibly means encouraging children to explore and share different methods of calculating and helping them appreciate that there is not necessarily one best method. This chapter looks at ways of helping children develop mental methods. Chapter 5 builds on this to explore paper and pencil methods.

National Curriculum expectations

The programme of study for number in the National Curriculum emphasises two aspects of calculating that children need to be taught.

First, there are various number facts that children need to commit to memory. At Key Stage 1 these include:

- addition and subtraction facts to 20;

- multiplication and division facts relating to the twos, fives, tens.

At Key Stage 2 pupils are expected to build on this knowledge and:

- consolidate addition and subtraction facts to 20;

- extend the multiplication and division facts to all pairs of numbers up to 10×10.

The second aspect of calculating is the ability to use these known number facts to find others. At Key Stage 1 children

- use mental methods to find, from known facts, number facts that they cannot recall;

- use these to learn other facts, for example use the known fact that $10 + 10 = 20$ to figure out that $10 + 11 = 21$ and eventually commit this to memory.

At Key Stage 2 children are expected to continue to build on their known number facts and

- develop a range of mental methods for figuring out quickly number facts that they cannot recall;

- extend the known facts that they use to include multiples, factors and squares, and eventually primes, cubes and square roots.

At both Key Stages children are expected to develop a variety of methods for calculating including:

- using the fact that subtraction is the inverse of addition (Key Stage 1);

- understanding multiplication as repeated addition, and division both as sharing and repeated subtraction (Key Stage 2);

- developing mental methods of computation with whole numbers up to 100 (Key Stage 2);

- developing a range of non-calculator methods of computation that involve addition and subtraction of whole numbers, multiplication and division of up to three-digit by two-digit whole numbers (Key Stage 2).

Children at Key Stage 1 are expected to be able to use a basic calculator and read the display, while at Key Stage 2 this needs to be extended to being able to interpret calculator answers in the context of the problem, including rounding and remainders.

The expectation is that by the end of Key Stage 2 children should be confident with a range of methods of computation that includes addition and subtraction with negative numbers, all four operations with decimals, and calculating fractions and percentages of quantities.

Teaching and learning about mental methods of computation

In developing mental methods of computation, attention has to be paid to two distinct aspects. First, there are mental methods of computation that are based on either instant or rapid recall of number facts. Having a repertoire of number facts, such as number bonds to 20 and multiplication facts to 10×10, is part of having a sound foundation in number. Later in this chapter I discuss ways in which pupils can be helped to commit these to memory.

The second aspect of mental mathematics that also has to be addressed is the ability of children to mentally figure out number calculations that they cannot rapidly recall. For example, it is unlikely that anyone would commit to memory the answer to $46 + 58$ but children who are confident in number should be able to find the answer mentally. As indicated the National Curriculum for mathematics emphasises that pupils need to be given opportunities to develop flexible methods of working with number, including mentally, and to develop mental methods that enable them to use known facts to derive facts that they cannot recall.

Known facts and derived facts

Research suggests that the two aspects of mental mathematics – known facts and derived facts – are complementary. Studies of arithmetical methods used by seven-to twelve-year-olds show that higher attaining pupils demonstrate the ability to use known number facts to figure out other number facts (Gray, 1991; Steffe, 1983) .

For example, a pupil may 'know by heart' that 5 + 5 = 10 and use this to 'figure out' that 5 + 6 must be 11, one more than 5 + 5. At a later stage, a pupil may know that 4×25 is 100 and use that to figure out that 40×24 must be 960.

The evidence suggests that pupils who are able to make these links between recalled and deduced number facts make good progress because each approach supports the other.

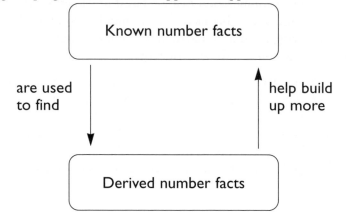

Eventually, some number facts that pupils previously deduced become known number facts and, in turn, as their range of known number facts expands so too does the range of strategies that they have available for deriving facts.

However, it is also clear that there are many children who, even by the end of primary school, rely more on procedures such as counting to find the answer to calculation and do not make as much progress.

At Key Stage 1 what might we expect children to know in terms of known number facts and what might we expect them to be able to deduce? At a minimum, children might be expected to be able to do the following by instant or rapid recall:

■ simple doubles up to 5 + 5;

■ adding and subtracting one from any number to 10;

■ number bonds to 10 (pairs of numbers that add up to 10);

■ being able to add 10 to any single-digit number.

Strategic approaches to addition and subtraction bonds to 10

There are 100 separate number facts in being able to answer every addition of pairs of numbers from 1 to 10. Unlike the 'times tables' we do not expect children to commit these to memory by chanting tables (the one plus table: one plus one is two, one plus two is three and so on). In being able to compute these 100 number facts children appear to go through four stages:

Counting all

In order to add, say 5 and 4, a child will count out five fingers or counters,

count out another four

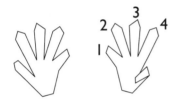

and then recount them all, starting with the first of the five

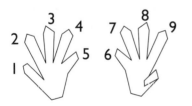

Counting on

Now the child will put out five fingers or counters and then another four but will count on without needing to recount the first five. Alternatively they put out five fingers and count on until they can see that they have put up four more fingers, but counting them as, six, seven, eight, nine.

A common error that children make at this stage is to start the counting on from the last finger or counter of the first group put out so that they end up with an answer that is one too small. For example, if they want to add 5 and 4, they put out five fingers. They start to count on 4 but begin on the fifth finger. They then end up with eight fingers raised, which they count.

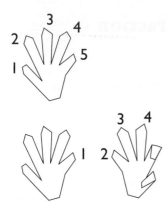

A strategy that helps children avoid this mistake and encourages them to move on from counting all is to encourage them to 'hold' the first number in their head. Get the children to 'put' five in their heads and hold it there by putting a hand on their head. Then they put out the fingers on their other hand as they count on and they are forced to start with the first finger of the second group rather than the last of the first.

Known facts

Some facts get quickly committed to memory. Notably simple doubles. Children also learn quickly to add 1, although the order in which the calculation is given may make a difference. A child who can quickly tell you that eight add one is nine may have to count on if asked what one add eight is.

Derived facts

This is when children can begin to figure out the answer by what they know rather than counting strategies. So a child who knows that five add five is ten may be able to figure out that five add four is one less, so must be nine.

Once children have begun to build up a repertoire of known facts and have some simple strategies for deriving facts they can begin to explore further strategies. For example:

- knowing the complements to 10: the pairs of numbers that add to 10
  2 + 8, 3 + 7 and so on

- being able to add 10 instantly to a single digit

- being able to rapidly add 9
  add 10 and take off one or take off one and add 10

- knowing the doubles to 10 + 10

- use the known double facts to rapidly find near doubles
  6 + 7 is one more than 6 + 6

- being able to 'bridge through 10'
  use knowledge of complements to partition a number to make bond to 10
  for example, 8 + 5 = 8 + 2 + 3

- using the commutative law
  2 + 8 = 8 + 2

Strategic approaches to addition and subtraction bonds to 20

Building on the above, strategies that Key Stage 1 children might use to deduce number facts up to 20 include:

■ rearranging the order of calculation, for example given 8 + 11, calculating 11 + 8;

■ rearranging the numbers, for example appreciating that 18 + 1 will give the same result as 11 + 8.

In Key Stage 2, assuming children are confident with the addition and subtraction bonds to 20, further strategies that they might use to help them mentally add any two two-digit numbers include:

■ partitioning both numbers into their component tens and ones, adding the tens, adding the ones and adding the two totals together:
  for example finding the answer to 38 + 27 by adding 30 and 20 to get 50, 8 and 7 to get 15 and finally adding the 50 and 15 to get 65;

■ keeping one number intact, and partitioning the other number into its component tens and ones, adding the tens to the intact number and then adding the ones:
  finding the answer to 38 + 27 using this method would mean adding 20 to 38 to get 58 and then adding on the 7 to get 65;

■ rounding one number to a multiple of 10 and either adjusting the second number or adjusting the answer:
  so 38 + 27 could be calculated by saying that this is the equivalent of 40 + 25 (rounding the 38 up to 40 and compensating for this by reducing the 27 by 2) or adding 40 and 27 to get 67 and then subtracting the 2.

Ten-ten or number-ten?

Which method children use for addition of two two-digit numbers may affect their ability to extend this into carrying out subtractions mentally.

The method that involves partitioning both numbers into their component tens and ones can be thought of as a ten-ten (TT) method.

The method that involves keeping one number intact, and partitioning the other number into its component tens and ones can be thought of as a number-ten (NT) method.

Here are the two methods applied to 45 + 33

- TT: 45 + 32 -> 40 + 30 = 70 -> 5 + 2 = 7 -> 70 + 7 = 77
- NT: 45 + 32 -> 45 + 30 = 75 -> 75 + 2 = 77

Use the ten-ten and the number-ten methods to find the answer to each of these additions in two different ways:

     53 + 26   48 + 29

Now try and adapt each method to calculate these subtractions in both fashions:

     58 - 24   43 - 29

Was either method easier to use for subtraction? If so, why do you think that was the case?

Research suggests that children who use the NT method find it easier to adapt this to subtraction problems than children who use the TT method (Beishuizen, 1995).

Assuming that pupils have been taught a sound understanding of the place value system a question is whether strategies for mental calculations can actively be taught to pupils or whether pupils develop them for themselves as a result of either maturation or experience?

While many pupils do succeed in learning mental strategies many others appear not to develop such confidence and facility. For example, by the time they reach secondary school, pupils unskilled in mental methods appear to:

- not look for the availability of alternative methods and overlook number properties that may be obvious to more skilled mental calculators;

- try and replicate paper and pencil methods in their heads.

One reason that some pupils do not learn strategic methods for mental mathematics would seem to arise out of an over-reliance on counting procedures. The work of Denvir demonstrated that many lower-attaining Key Stage 2 pupils relied mainly on counting strategies based on objects (fingers or counters) or representations of objects (Denvir, 1984). Other strong evidence in research indicates that, right into Key Stage 3, some pupils do not progress far beyond developing arithmetic techniques that rely on early number skills, such as 'counting on' instead of addition or relying on repeated addition for multiplication (Hart, 1981).

For some lower-attaining pupils it appears that over-dependence on counting methods, while leading to a correct result, removes the need to commit number facts to memory, which in turn limits their development in strategic methods.

Can mental methods be taught?

Research does show that children can be taught mental strategies.

One project looked at strategies for encouraging Year 3 pupils to move on from relying on inefficient techniques to solve numerical problems (for example counting in one's) to using known and derived facts (Askew, Bibby and Brown, 1997). A central principle to this work was to identify known number facts that the pupils were confident in and build on these to derive other number facts and to actively discourage the pupils from using counting methods.

Another research study that worked with nine and eleven year-olds on explicitly raising their awareness of mental strategies found that as well as developing the ability to use many different non-standard methods pupils also appeared to have a better understanding of

- place value;
- number decomposition;
- order of operations;
- number properties;

(Markovits and Sowder, 1988)

Mental arithmetic is generally perceived as being done without recording, paper and pencil to be used only when a calculation cannot be carried out in the head. However, it seems that some recording – jottings – helps children to learn mental strategies.

Ben

Ben (Year 3) knew that 4 + 4 = 8 but was unable to make the link that 4 + 5 must be 9.

Every time Ben was asked to do a calculation he treated it as a new situation to be worked out afresh, so rather than using his knowledge of 4 + 4 to find the answer to 4 + 5 he wanted to use a counting method (Askew, Bibby and Brown, 1997).

The key to solving Ben's difficulty was to get him to make some intermediate recording. He was asked to place four counters in each of two pots and record the situation, a known fact which he could do.

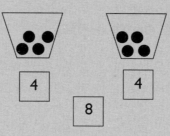

Ben's known fact

Ben was asked to add another counter to one of the pots and to say if the number cards were still correct. Ben not only knew that they were not but was able to 'correct' the recording to match the new situation. He could then do that without recalculating the total but by using his recorded known fact.

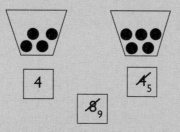

Ben's derived fact

Having made this connection the teacher reported a marked change in Ben's attitude and approach to mathematics, demonstrating an awareness that it was something he could do in his head rather than having to rely on external counting materials.

The use of an 'empty' number line as discussed in Chapter 3 would seem to be a valuable intermediate recording tool in helping pupils to develop mental strategies.

From paper and pencil to mental methods

275 seven-year-old pupils were assessed using an 'arithmetic scrap-paper test' where pupils were asked to write down their solution steps in a 'scrap-paper box' alongside the answer to the problem so that methods and strategies could be analysed. (Beishuizen, 1995). Between April and June there was evidence of changes in the strategies pupils used, with less emphasis on the empty number line. For example, in April a pupil typically answered 42 + 43 = using a blank number line:

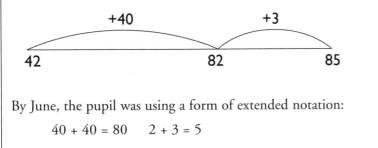

By June, the pupil was using a form of extended notation:

40 + 40 = 80   2 + 3 = 5

80 + 5 = 85

To summarise, teaching that is focused on mental mathematics is important for several reasons:

- it helps children make links between what they know (known number facts) and what they do not know (derived number facts);

- it helps emphasise that learning mathematics is about methods as much as it is about getting the right answers;

- explaining how you worked something out is a powerful way of learning, far more effective than being told how to work it out;

- it helps children realise that there is more than one way to work things out;

- it builds children's confidence and helps them realise that mathematics is something to be worked on, not something that some people can just do and others cannot.

The power of presentation

Askew, *et al* (1997) gives an example of a class of Year 2 children working on strategies for adding 9 to a two-digit number. The teacher asked if anyone had a short-cut method. Two suggestions were offered: adding 10 and then subtracting 1 and subtracting 1 and then adding10. The teacher offered the children several examples to work out using whichever method they preferred. By the end of this part of the lesson the majority of children in the class were happy using one or other of the short-cuts to add 9.

The teacher then directed the children to a page in a text book which had several examples of adding 9 to practise, but each was presented as a vertical calculation.

$$
\begin{array}{r}
36 \\
+\ \underline{9} \\
\end{array}
$$

Most of the children abandoned the method they had been using and reverted to adding the units, including going back to counting on 9 on their fingers. Several of the children even asked the teacher if they should do these like 'proper sums'.

Why does the way a calculation is presented encourage children to use particular methods?

How can children be encouraged to make calculations 'their own' and work them out in a way that is efficient and effective regardless of how they are presented?

Strategic approaches to multiplication and division facts to 10 × 10

While some children do benefit a great deal from learning the multiplication tables, it is important that they can deal flexibly with the information in the tables. For example, the child that knows that 3 × 8 = 24, should also be able to figure out from this that

8 × 3 = 24

24 ÷ 8 = 3

24 ÷ 3 = 8

Unfortunately, for many children, too much emphasis on simply chanting (or as is fashionable, singing) the tables can lead to 3 × 8 and 8 × 3 being seen as completely separate with no connection to the division facts being made at all.

Times or timesed by?

How do you 'read' 3 × 4? Try to give this to a few friends and see what they say.

Most people 'read' this as 'three times four'. In other words you start off with a group of four and take it three times.

The other way to 'read' 3 × 4 is 'three timesed by four' or 'three multiplied by four'.
Does it make any difference which of these two 'readings' you use?

The advantage of the second reading is that it is consistent with the way we usually 'read' the other rules of arithmetic, as 'take a number and then operate on it with the operation that follows'.
So 3 + 4 is 'three add four' – start with three and operate on it. Similarly with 10 – 6 we start with ten and perform the operation of subtraction on it. And 12 ÷ 4 is 'twelve divided by four', so start with 12 and operate on it with division. Three multiplied by four is consistent with the mathematics of the other three operations and is the 'reading' that we are assuming here.

Children need to be secure in knowing triples – 3, 8, 24; 6, 7, 42 – the sets of three numbers that are multiplicatively linked together. To help build up a sound knowledge of the triples the multiplication facts can be worked on strategically, in the same way that the addition facts to 20 can be worked on strategically. The key ideas to introduce the children to include are:

- commutativity;

- doubles and double doubles;

- square numbers;

- multiplying by 10;

- counting in fives and threes;

- the pattern of nines.

Commutativity

The fact that multiplication is commutative (the order of the numbers leaves the answer unchanged, for example, 3 × 4 = 4 × 3) immediately reduces by half the number of multiplication facts to commit to memory. To help children appreciate this it is useful to use the area model for multiplication: arrays of counters, rows of pegs on a pegboard, rectangles on squared paper.

The advantage of these images is that they can be rotated through 90° to demonstrate that the total is unchanged. The other popular 'model' for multiplication is repeated addition: 3 x 4 is three lots of four. In this model, it is slightly less obvious that 3 x 4 is the same as 4 x 3.

Doubling

Being able to double gives the two times table.

Double doubling

Doubling, and then doubling again, provides a strategic approach to multiplying by 4.

Square numbers

Just as knowing the doubles is a key foundation in committing addition facts to memory, so knowing the square numbers – 1×1, 2×2, 3×3 and so on to 10×10 – is a cornerstone in the multiplication facts. Again, working with arrays can help children commit these to memory and explore the number patterns.

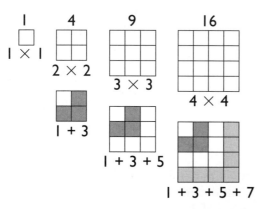

Multiplying by 10

Children should know instantly how to multiply a single-digit number by 10. Although they might decide that the short-cut method is to add a nought, as a teacher you should avoid telling the children this (the rule does not hold for multiplying decimal numbers). Instead, point out to them that multiplying by 10 makes everything ten times bigger and so the numbers move up a column in the place value table.

Counting in fives and the pattern of the multiples of five

The pattern of fives needs to be frequently explored by counting on in fives, halving multiples of 10 and so on.

Counting in threes

The are no real short-cuts to learning the pattern of multiples of threes. Children simply need to frequently rehearse it.

It is helpful to examine the pattern that the multiples of three make: if the 'digital root' is found, add the single digits (and then digits in the answer if it has more than one digit) until a single digit is reached, then the answer should be 3, 6, or 9.

3		3
6		6
9		9
12	1 + 2	3
15	1 + 5	6
...		
27	2 + 7	9

The patterns of nines

One way of exploring this is to multiply by 10 and subtract the number being multiplied. So 9 x 4 is 40 − 4 = 36; 9 × 8 = 80 − 8 = 72.

Finger multiplication for multiplying by 9 appeals to children.

Hold out both hands palms up and mentally label the fingers and thumbs from 1 to 10 starting at the far left.

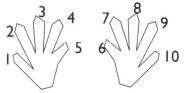

Bend towards you the finger that has the value you want to multiply by 9, say 7.

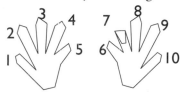

The number of fingers to the left of the bent finger is the number of tens in the answer. In this case, six.

The number of fingers to the right of the bent finger is the number of ones in the answer. Here there are three.

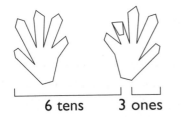

6 tens   3 ones

So nine times seven is sixty-three.

Like the pattern of multiples of three, the pattern of the digital roots of multiples of nine provides a useful check that the answer obtained really is a multiple of nine.

9		9
18	1 + 8	9
27	2 + 7	9
36	3 + 6	9
...		
81	8 + 1	9

With the above in place the tables can easily be strategically reconstructed if children forget them (in order of difficulty):

$\times$ 2 double

$\times$ 4 double and double again

$\times$ 10 place value

$\times$ 5 pattern of fives or $\times$ 10 and half

$\times$ 9 pattern of nines

$\times$ 3 counting in threes

$\times$ 6 $\times$ 3 and double.

What about the sevens and eights? Well, if children know that multiplication is commutative, then most of the 7 and 8 tables' facts can be 'turned around'. So 7×5 becomes 5×7. Only three facts are not covered by this: 7×7, 8×8 and 7×8. The first two of these are covered by knowing the square numbers. As for 7×8, well you just have to remember it. It's the table fact that everyone has most difficulty with.

Managing mental mathematics sessions

All the above suggests that at any point in time a particular child will be at three different levels of mental mathematics: she will have a bank of 'known facts', a bank of number facts that she can figure out (that may or may not eventually become known facts) and a range of strategies for figuring out derived facts.

Now, put 20 or 30 children together and the overlap between these three areas is probably pretty small. What is a known fact for one child will be a derived fact for another, and the strategy that one child uses for a derived fact may be quicker and more efficient than that used for another child. So, pose a mental arithmetic question and the likelihood that everyone will answer in the same length of time is pretty small.

This raises questions about how best to manage mental arithmetic sessions so that as many children as possible are fully engaged. The traditional method of asking a question and waiting for the volley of hands to go up does have several drawbacks:

- it emphases the rapid, the known, over the derived – those children who 'know' the answer invariably beat those who still have to figure it out;

- it is unhelpful to those figuring out – you just start collecting your thoughts when you are distracted by all this movement, straining to raise hands high and mutterings of 'me' or 'miss';

- children learn to play the system and avoid really taking part either by putting their hands up quickly (teacher never picks those children whose hands go up first) or waiting until there are sufficient hands up to hide quietly behind them;

- it makes it hard for the teacher to choose anyone who isn't straining to give the answer.

The result is that those who already can do it are rewarded, while those who cannot do not get the opportunity to really practise the calculation.

The trick for the teacher is to find ways to provide some thinking time (but not an endless amount). Strategies that can be successful include:

- insisting that NOBODY puts a hand up until you give the signal and silently counting to five or ten before giving the signal;

- getting children to simply raise a finger to indicate that they are ready to answer and explaining that this is so as not to disturb the others;

- insisting that everybody keeps as still as possible, that not even by raising an eyebrow should anyone indicate that they think they have the answer;

■ providing 'chained' calculations: 'put five in your heads, double it *(pause)* add two *(pause)* take off five *(pause)* OK'. By varying the number of links in the chain children never know at what point you are going to say OK, and so hands all go up together.

A way of being able to match questions to individuals is to use end of sessions time to sharpen mental arithmetic skills: when children are lined up to leave the classroom asking each one a question in turn or sending them off one at a time when they correctly answer a question.

It is a good idea in these circumstances to have a specific focus. That can help the less confident children get the answers by listening to and building on the answers of the more confident children. For example, a class may be being dismissed by finding complements to 100. So one child may be asked what the complement of 68 is and you might immediately follow this by asking another child the complement of 78.

ACTIVITY 1 *Six grid*

This activity is designed to help introduce children to multiplication using the area model. It helps them see patterns in the numbers and relate the multiplication facts to an image of areas of rectangles. Children who are still at the counting stage will be able to engage with the task and should benefit from others who may be beginning to use multiplication facts.

Organisation

Each child will need a six by six grid of squares, each square being large enough for them to easily write in a two-digit number. The top left-hand corner of the grid should be marked with a dot. They will also need an L-shaped piece of card with a dot in the inner corner of the L.

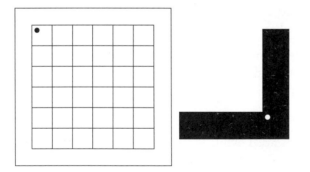

If possible, it is helpful for you to have transparencies like this to demonstrate to the children what to do on an overhead projector.

ACTIVITY 1   Six grid (Continued)

Starting off

In a large group, give the children a simple 'story' problem that could be solved by multiplication in their heads. For example:

Sam and Jo and their Mum and Dad went to a Chinese restaurant. They all used chopsticks. How many chopsticks did they need?

Discourage children from calling out the answer or vying to be chosen. Instead invite two or three children to explain how they worked it out. It is likely that some children will have used repeated addition while others may have used multiplication. Encourage the children to offer as many different solution methods as possible.

Record the different methods that the children used on the board and discuss why they all give the same answer.

Developing the activity

Give each child a blank grid and L-shape. Show them how to position their grid so that the dot is in the top left-hand corner. Demonstrate that they are to make rectangles by placing the L-shape on the grid so that the dot on the L is diagonally opposite the one on the grid, that is in the bottom right-hand corner.

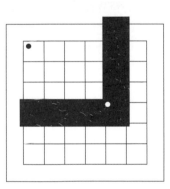

Ask the children to find out how many small squares there are in the rectangle that they have marked out and to write the total in the square next to the dot on the L-shape.

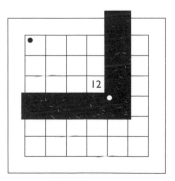

ACTIVITY 1 Six grid (Continued)

The children's task is to carry on moving the L-shape, marking off rectangles in the same way and filling in all the areas. It is likely that you will have to respond to questions about whether or not marking off a square counts as a rectangle.

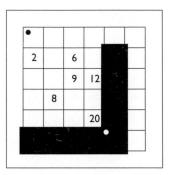

Sharing outcomes

Invite children to talk about how they completed the task. The children are likely to have used four different strategies:

- counted every square in the rectangle;

- repeated addition, so, for example, a rectangle 4 wide by 3 deep could be seen as three rows of four, so 4 + 4 + 4;

- using the patterns that emerge: the third row contains 3, 6, 9 so the next entry is 12;

- using multiplication: knowing that 3 × 4 is 12.

If all four strategies do not emerge from the children then introduce and explain them yourself. Discuss with the children which strategy they think is the best.

Now direct the children's attention to the completed grids. What patterns can they find? Can they find the even numbers? Look at the row with 5 at the front. What do they notice? Where else on the grid can they find this pattern of fives?

Show the children how to use the grid to multiply two numbers together by placing a finger on a number in the top row, say 4, and a number on the left column, say 5, and sliding these until they meet, in this case at 20.

Encourage the children to study the grid and try and remember the patterns.

Questions to ask

- What do you think the next number in that row is going to be?

- Can you see a pattern down that column?

- If the grid was seven by seven is there a quick way of finding the missing numbers?

- Look at the numbers on the diagonal down from the dot. What is special about these numbers?

ACTIVITY 1 Six grid (Continued)

Providing for differentiation

The activity itself allows for differentiation in that the children can approach it in several different ways.

Children who complete the task quickly, using an efficient strategy, can be encouraged to extend the size of the grid to ten by ten.

Children who count all the squares should be encouraged to use repeated addition. They can be helped in this by providing them with another piece of card that can be used to cover up squares so that only one row at a time is visible.

Assessment opportunities

As the children work on the task observe how they are going about it. Is anyone being systematic in the way they mark off rectangles? Is anyone using the number patterns that emerge to make the task easier? Is anyone using multiplication bonds to find the answers? Make a mental note of who you are going to invite to make a contribution in the feedback time.

Communication

Getting the children to explain clearly and carefully to each other how they filled in the grid.

Progression

Over time give the children multiplication calculations to work out using their grids. As the children become more proficient, encourage them to try and work out the answer in their heads first. One approach is to get them to place their grids face down in front of them. Give them the calculation to do and allow them a few seconds before they can turn over their grids to check if they were correct.

Consolidation

- Get the children to cut up completed grids into nine two by two squares. How quickly can they put their 'jigsaw' back together?

- Give the children a multiplication grid with half the numbers blanked out.

1			4	5	
2		6			12
	6	9	12		18
	8			20	
5			20	25	
	12	18		30	

Can they put this back together when it is cut into two by two squares?
Then, taking each two by two square individually, can they fill in the blanks?

- Get the children to shade in on their grids the multiplication facts that they have committed to memory.

ACTIVITY 1 *Six grid (Continued)*

Links within the mathematics curriculum

- Use the grid to explore factors: how many times does, say, 20 appear? Are there any other pairs of numbers that multiply together to make 20 that are not on the grid?

- Use the grid to explore prime numbers. Ignoring the numbers in the top row and left column, strike out on a number line or 1 to 36 number square the numbers that appear in the 'body' of the multiplication square. Which numbers do not get struck out? Why not?

Links across the curriculum

- Look out for opportunities to discuss when multiplication is useful. For example when there are several groups all containing the same number of items: the total number of items when several packets of 'multi-buys' are purchased; teams in a tournament; packets of stickers. Or when items are arranged in arrays: vegetables in gardens, seats at a concert, stamps on a sheet.

ACTIVITY 2   *What else do I know?*

This is activity is designed to focus children's attention on derived number facts. By working with numbers that are too large to be dealt with directly, strategies for deriving information can be discussed.

Organisation

This requires very little advance preparation. Children will need paper and pencil to record.

Starting off

Put a calculation on the board that children will not know by heart and where the numbers are too large to be able to work with using counting strategies. For example:

$50 \times 40 = 2\,000$.

Ask the children to use this information to work out 51×40. Encourage them to work mentally. Invite individuals to explain their reasoning behind the answer. Continue presenting calculations that can be derived from this one basic 'fact' and discussing the strategy for finding the answer, for example:

49×40

50×41

50×400

50×39

51×39

500×400

$2\,000 \div 50$

$2\,000 \div 39$

5×3.9

150×40

25×40

75×40

Developing the activity

Get the children to work in pairs. Give each pair a 'core' calculation and answer and ask them to create as many new calculations and answers as they can, the answer to which can be derived from their core calculation.

ACTIVITY 2 *What else do I know? (Continued)*

Sharing outcomes

Invite pairs of children to present their lists of calculations to the rest of the class. They could do this by presenting the core and new calculations and challenging the class to find the answers. Do they agree with the answers the pair arrived at? Can anyone suggest some other calculations, the answer to which could be derived from the core calculation?

Questions to ask

What happens to the answer if you increase that number by 1?
What happens to the answer if you double that number?
What happens to the answer if you make that number one hundred times bigger?
What happens to the answer if you make that number ten times smaller?

Providing for differentiation

The activity is designed to allow for differentiation both by task and outcome. The 'core' calculation given to pairs of children can be altered to be easier or harder either by changing the size of the numbers or by altering the operation. Since the children are determining the calculations they can derive, this allows for differentiation by outcome.

Assessment opportunities

As the children work on the activity watch out for:

■ use of knowledge of place value to help create new calculations;

■ knowledge of the fact that subtraction and addition are inverse operations as are multiplication and division;

■ children being able to reason through the effect of making one number larger and the other smaller;

■ children appreciating the difference made by increasing the size of a number by multiplying it as opposed to adding something to it.

Communication

Children should be able to clearly explain the reasoning behind their answers. They should also be able to listen carefully and follow someone else's explanation and explain why they disagree with it if they think the conclusion is incorrect.

Progression

As children become familiar with the form of the activity, make it more challenging by introducing:

■ decimal numbers;

■ fractions;

■ percentages.

ACTIVITY 2   *What else do I know? (Continued)*

Consolidation

- Give the children a speed test: a core calculation is provided and they have, say, one minute to complete ten derived calculations.

- Give the children a series of calculations that could be derived from a nearby 'nice' calculation. For example, 49×11; 25×16.

- Challenge the children to make up their own core calculation and related calculations.

Links within the mathematics curriculum

The basic form of the activity is suitable for use in any aspect of the mathematics curriculum where there are calculations to be carried out: whole numbers, negative numbers, fractions, decimals, percentages, money and so on.

Links across the curriculum

The idea of being given one item of information and asking what else it is reasonable to deduce from this idea can be introduced in other aspects of the curriculum. For example, being told:

all mammals have a back bone

which of the following statements can reasonably be deduced:

a creature without a back bone cannot be a mammal;

a creature with a back bone must be a mammal;

a creature that is not a mammal cannot have a backbone.

Activities for developing knowledge of number bonds

Spill the beans

Ask the children to work in pairs. Each pair has a yoghurt pot and a specific number of dried beans: 10 or 20 depending on their level of attainment.

The children take it in turns to put all the beans in the pot and then turn it upside down, so that some beans spill out onto the table and some are trapped under the pot. The other child has to work out how many beans are hidden under the pot.

Can they record their results in an appropriate way?

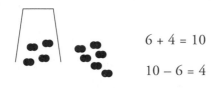

6 + 4 = 10

10 − 6 = 4

Ten fish

Prepare a set of fish cards: each card has the outline of a fish drawn on the front and the back. Each fish has a number of spots on it, the total of the two sides being 10 (or 20). Work with the children on showing them one side of the fish. Can they tell you how many spots you can see on the other side?

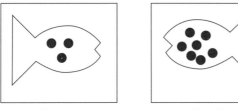

Front   Back

Hide some

Prepare for pairs of children a small collection of number cards, say numbered from 8 to 15. They also need a container of counters or small counting objects.

One child looks away. The other child turns over the top card and counts out that number of counters. She then hides some counters in her hand. For example she might turn over a card with 12 on and hides four counters in her hand, leaving eight on the table.

Her partner turns around and using the number of counters visible and the number on the card, has to figure out how many counters are hidden. Encourage the children to record their results.

Activities for developing knowledge of the tables

Triples

Prepare a set of 'triple' cards: cards with three numbers that are multiplicatively linked, for example, 3, 8, 24.

3	
	24
8	

Explain to the children the way the three numbers are linked.

Hold up a card facing the children, but with one of the numbers covered up. Can they figure out what the missing number is?

Give sets of triple cards to pairs or small groups of children. Ask them the write down all the number sentences that they can that link these three numbers. For example

$3 \times 8 = 24$

$8 \times 3 = 24$

$24 \div 8 = 3$

$24 \div 3 = 8$

(all these activities can also be done with cards made using addition triples).

Rectangles

Prepare sets of number cards from 1 to 36 and provide collections of counters.

In pairs, children turn over one of the number cards and take that number of counters. How many different rectangles can they make with the total number of counters? Discuss with the children whether a rectangle that is, say, 2 by 8 is different from one which is 8 by 2.

Ask them to record the different rectangles as multiplication facts. For example 12 can produce three different rectangles (assuming the children have agreed that rotating a rectangle through 90° does not produce a different one.)

$3 \times 4 = 12$

$2 \times 6 = 12$

$1 \times 12 = 12$

ACTIVITY BANK FOR MENTAL METHODS (Continued)

Empty number line jumps

Pairs or small groups of children will need a set of 1 to 10 number cards and a die. They roll the die and turn over one number card. The number on the die tells them how many jumps to make, the number on the card tells them how big the jumps should be. Children individually draw an empty number line and use it to work out how far the total of the jumps takes them. They compare answers and agree the result before rolling the die and selecting a card again.

For example, they roll 4 and select 8.

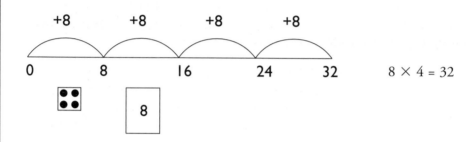

$8 \times 4 = 32$

Sandwiches

Give the children the following, or a similar problem.

Jo's cafe makes sandwiches with four different fillings:

   Ham, cheese, turkey or beef.

There are three different breads:

   Brown, white or granary.

How many different possible sandwiches are there?

Encourage the children to be systematic in the way that they record their results.
They should find that there are 12 different sandwiches. How does this relate to the fact that there were four fillings and three breads? Ask the children to make up similar problems and swap these with a friend to work out.

Other situations that can be used that lead to this experience of multiplication include:

■ flavours of ice-cream and toppings;

■ tee shirts and jeans;

■ different flowers and vases.

Activities for practising mental methods

Round the world

Invite one child to stand behind the chair of his neighbour. Pose a mental arithmetic question appropriate to the level of the pair of children. They race to call out the answer. If the child standing correctly answers first then he moves on to the next person. If the child sitting down gets the correct answer he swaps places with the child who is standing and moves on to the next person. Continue asking questions until you are back to the starting point.

Who moved most places? Can anyone get 'all round the world', that is back to his original chair?

(This is a game that pitches children against each other in pairs, so while being encouraged to be quick, children can take their time. The rest of the group are still involved. It's like playing *Trivial Pursuits* – you do try and answer the questions even when it isn't your turn.)

Beat the calculator

In pairs, the winner is the best of three calculations. A pair comes to the front and one of them HAS to use a calculator to find the answer, even if she can do it in her head. You will have to be a strong referee to make sure the child using the calculator does not call out the answer before she has keyed it in.

Prepared mental arithmetic tests

Write out and duplicate the questions before the lesson. Give the questions to the children who have, say, ten minutes to work on them – encourage them to sort out which questions they 'know' the answer to and which they need to figure out.

Spend some time talking with the class about the strategies they used and discuss which are most efficient.

Collect the papers in and then give children the test: read out the same questions but in a different order.

The one-minute tables test

Warn the children in advance that they are going to be given a mental arithmetic test and tell them which table they are individually going be tested on. Different children can be challenged on different tables according to their levels of attainment. Duplicate for each child ten randomly ordered 'multiplied by' questions that do not specify which table is being tested:

❏ × 3 =

❏ × 7 =

❏ × 5 =

and so on.

Give out the papers and get the children to write on the top which table they are using. They have exactly one minute to work out as many of the answers as they can, imagining that each box contains the value of the table they have learnt.

5

DEVELOPING CHILDREN'S UNDERSTANDING OF THE FOUR RULES OF ARITHMETIC

Introduction

Lizzie was working on finding the difference between the area of two feet. One covered 126 squares while another occupied 107. She wrote down

$$
\begin{array}{r}
126 \\
-107 \\
\hline
121 \\
\hline
\end{array}
$$

and was quite happy with her answer. Even when the teacher asked her to explain, Lizzie still did not think that anything was amiss. Lizzie only began to consider whether or not her answer was sensible when her teacher said 'So if you had £126 and I had £107 you are telling me that you would have £121 more than me?'

Many children, as they grow older, like Lizzie, come to see school problems as about moving marks around on the page and cease to try and make sense of the numbers involved. This chapter looks at some of the reasons why children find it difficult to 'make sense' of calculations and strategies for helping them develop better understandings.

National Curriculum expectations

The Programmes of Study do not make explicit mention of particular paper and pencil methods. Rather, children are expected to develop a variety of methods of calculation that extend mental methods and do not involve calculators. The implication is therefore that such methods would involve paper and pencil.

There is a distinction to be made between using paper and pencil as a means of recording methods of working and as a written method of calculation. The former includes making notes to support mental methods: the National Curriculum Programmes of Study explicitly indicate that opportunities need to be provided for children to record working in relation to mental methods.

Written methods of calculation in contrast refer to calculations which are too large or complicated to do mentally, even with some intermediate written 'jottings'. So while a child might be confident in adding two two-digit numbers mentally, she might choose to use a written method to add a string of five two-digit numbers. Of course, written methods also require mental calculation.

Teaching and learning about the meaning of the four operations

Too often the emphasis in primary mathematics is on children being able to find the answer to calculations. While it is important that they can calculate efficiently and effectively, if children can only carry out a calculation when it is specified for them what calculation to do, then they are not being helped to become numerate.

Who's doing the mathematics?

Mark, Year 2, had been given a page from a scheme to do which was about finding the difference. At the top of the page was a diagram like this:

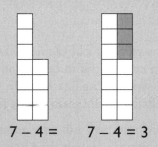

$$7 - 4 = \qquad 7 - 4 = 3$$

The page contained diagrams of similar pairs of towers of squares and the instruction to write the 'sum' and find the answer.

Mark was stuck and talking to him it was clear that he was having difficulty 'reading' the diagram as a subtraction, as to him it showed that $4 + 3 = 7$.

He took the page to his teacher who told him just to write down the 'take-away' that each pair of towers made. Happy that he now knew what to do, Mark successfully completed the page (Askew, 1989).

- To what extent do you think Mark's understanding of finding the difference was helped by the teacher's strategy?

- Who had to make sense of the mathematics in this situation?

- How would you have helped Mark make the connection between the diagrams and the calculation?

The mathematical operations of addition, subtraction, multiplication and division can be represented through at least five different 'modes' of representations:

- a calculation in figures;

- a calculation in words;

This example has been discussed at length, not because you will need to teach children how to divide fractions, but because it illustrates some of the understandings children have to develop in order to be confident in making sense of calculations. It demonstrates that there is more to understanding arithmetical operations than simply getting the right answer.

In order to be confident in the four operations, children need to be able to move easily between these different modes of representation. One of the difficulties that children have in becoming confident in understanding the operations is that they do not appreciate that one single expression of a calculation in figures can lead to several different other modes of representation.

Half a person?

Anghileri (1995) gives the example of two Year 6 girls, Lisa and Anna, who are trying to find an answer to 6 000 ÷ 6 =. They used their table facts to solve problems like 28 ÷ 7 = and 35 ÷ 5 = and had interpreted the question as 'How many sixes are there in six thousand?'. They had gathered together enough structured rods and blocks to represent six thousand and were 'taking away' groups of six. This was clearly going to take them a long time to solve.

Even though Lisa and Anna had put their apparatus out in six piles, each representing 1 000 'ones', the teacher was not able to help them 'read' 6 000 ÷ 6 as six thousand shared by 6, the solution to which was already in front of them.

On the other hand, Lorraine and Jody (Year 6) had successfully used the phrase 'shared by' to find answers to questions like 12 ÷ 3 =, 20 ÷ 4 = and 28 ÷ 7 =.

Being presented with 6 ÷ ½ = reduced them to fits of giggles as they could not see any way of making sense of how to share 6 with 'half a person'.

In contrast to Lisa and Anna, Lorraine and Jody had read the division as a shared by problem but this was no help to them. Had they been able to 'read' the calculation as 'how many halves are there in 6' they would have made a different sense of it and possibly found a solution.

In its pure form, each calculation that the girls were stuck on was of the same form: one number divided by another. Being able to 'read' the calculation is not simply a case of deciding what the division symbol stands for. It involves looking at the numbers, together with the division sign, and deciding which 'reading' makes most sense.

As Anghileri's research shows, once children have chosen a particular way to 'read' a calculation it is difficult to switch to other readings. But unless they can successfully do this, then, like Lisa, Anna, Lorraine and Jody, they may end up using very inefficient methods or not even being able to start. As this example shows, it is not simply the case that children have to 'make sense' of a calculation, they also have to decide which 'sense' to make.

There are two lessons here for the teacher:

■ Do not place too much emphasis on one practical model for an operation. It is easy, for example, to provide children with a diet of lots of practical experience of subtraction as 'taking away' because this is the easiest way to model subtraction using cubes.

Similarly you need to watch out for always presenting division as 'shared by' problems. It is important that children get experiences of all the different interpretations of the operations of arithmetic.

■ Watch your own language when reading calculations to children. If you always 'read' subtraction problems as 'take-aways' for example 12 − 5 = is 'twelve take away five', then children are likely to interpret the subtraction symbol as only able to be read as a take-away.

Some teachers argue that 'subtraction' is too difficult a word for young children, but they handle words like television or video-recorder which are just as complicated. If you do not like 'subtraction' then 'minus' also does not have the connotations of only being related to one specific physical action.

Developing children's understanding of addition and subtraction

Consider, for example, the subtraction calculation 12 − 7 =. This can be 'read' in words in many different ways, including:

■ What is twelve minus seven?

■ What is twelve subtract seven?

■ What is twelve take away seven?

■ What is seven less than twelve?

■ How many more than seven is twelve?

■ How many less than twelve is seven?

■ What is the difference between twelve and seven?

One way that appears to be successful in helping children appreciate the idea of an operation being 'read' in several different ways is through working on problems in a range of different realistic contexts. The children can find solutions to the problems in whatever way they like and then are taught how they can be recorded mathematically. So right from an early age they are introduced to the idea that one operation symbol can stand for lots of different actions.

Here are some examples of how simple situations can then provide a range of story problems, the operations that children might use and some of the different ways that they can be recorded mathematically.

Bus-stops

■ Five people are on a bus and eight more get on. How many people are on the bus? (Addition: 5 + 8 = ❑)

■ Some people are on a bus and eight get off at a stop. Now there are five people on the bus. How many people were on the bus to start off with? (Addition: 8 + 5 = ❑; subtraction: ❑ − 8 = 5)

Ratio and proportion

Research suggests that children who do not have an image of multiplication and division as representing scalings may have difficulty with ideas of ratio and proportion later on.

Hart (1981) gives the example of pupils being given this rectangle:

3cm

2cm

The pupils were asked to complete this diagram so that it was the same shape but larger than the one above.

5cm

To answer this successfully, the pupils had to realise that the length of 3cm had been scaled up in the ration of 5 : 3. So the length of the missing side had to be calculated by multiplying 2 by 5 and dividing by 3.

Only 20% of a large sample of 11-to 16-year-olds tested could do this.

The most common error that the pupils made was to use an addition strategy: 2 needs to be added to 3 to make 5, so add 2 to the 2cm.

There is one final model for multiplication that does not have an equivalent in division: multiplication as a Cartesian product. This is best illustrated by an example.

■ Jenni has 3 tee-shirts and 4 pairs of shorts. How many different outfits can she wear?

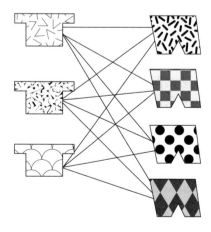

By carefully matching each tee-shirt with each pair of shorts, it can be seen that 12 different combinations are possible: $3 \times 4 = 12$.

Similarly, if sandwiches are made with three types of bread and five different fillings, there are 15 possible combinations.

Teaching and learning about written methods for calculation

In a now classic article, Plunkett (1979) compared mental calculation methods with standard written algorithms. The latter are useful in terms of efficiency, automaticity and generality but do not correspond to mental methods which are flexible and use complete numbers.

The strength of vertical written methods lies in their effectiveness – correctly used they give right answers. However, they are not always the most efficient method to use. A written algorithm for finding the answer to 7426 – 4679 is likely to be efficient and effective, but a mental method is more appropriate and efficient for 34 – 27.

Subtractions

A Year 6 class were asked to find the difference between 1736 and 5863. Here are Rumen's and Anthea's working.

$$
\begin{array}{r}
5 8 \overset{5\,1}{\cancel{6}} 3 \\
-1736 \\
\hline
4127
\end{array}
\qquad
\begin{array}{r}
5863 \\
-1736 \\
\hline
1800 \\
2000 \\
5863
\end{array}
\qquad
\begin{array}{r}
64 \\
200 \\
3863 \\
\hline
4063 \\
4127
\end{array}
$$

If you are familiar with the decomposition method it is fairly clear what Rumen did, but Anthea's jottings are less explicit. When the teacher asked Anthea to explain her method to the class she said, 'Well sixty-four and thirty-six makes a hundred, so that's one thousand eight hundred, another two hundred makes two thousand. I need another three thousand eight hundred and sixty-three, so that's four thousand and sixty-three plus the sixty-four is four thousand one hundred and twenty seven.'

Finding effective methods means helping children realise, among other things, that they need to consider the size and type of numbers involved when selecting a method. Trying to subtract 1 999 from 2 001 by decomposition is not only inefficient but likely to lead to an incorrect answer. Searching for my calculator to work out 372 × 428 might be sensible, but using it to find 372 × 500 should not be necessary if I appreciate that I can easily find 372 × 1 000 and halve the answer.

Appropriate methods of calculation

Make up some calculations using the four rules of arithmetic: addition, subtraction, multiplication and division.

The numbers involved should all be at least two-digit numbers and you should feel confident that you could find the answers using a mental method of calculation.

Now make up some similar calculations, but this time ones that make you feel you would *need* to use paper and pencil to find the answer.

Finally, make up some calculations that you feel you would make you *want* to use a calculator for finding the answer.

What decisions were guiding your choice of size and type of number for each of the four operations?

Traditionally, the emphasis in primary school mathematics has been on teaching children effective methods. Text books provide pages of subtraction calculations and children are expected to work out the answers using the same method, irrespective of the size of numbers involved or how confident they feel with different methods.

Playing the game

I sat down next to Leah (Year 4) who was coming to the end of working out a page of subtraction calculations. Each one was set out as vertical calculation and it was clear that the pupils were expected to find the answer using decomposition. However, I could see that Leah was finding the answer mentally and I asked her to explain her thinking. A typical calculation was

$$
\begin{array}{r}
83 \\
-56 \\
\hline
\end{array}
$$

Leah: *Well, fifty-six add four is sixty, another twenty is eighty, so that's twenty-four, and three more is eighty-three so that's twenty-seven. The answer is twenty-seven.*

She wrote down
$$
\begin{array}{r}
83 \\
-56 \\
\hline
27
\end{array}
$$

As I walked away I noticed that Leah was going back over what she had written down to make it look like each calculation had been done using decomposition:

$$\begin{array}{r} \overset{6}{\cancel{8}}\overset{1}{3} \\ -\ 5\ 6 \\ \hline 2\ 7 \end{array}$$

I asked her why.

'*Well,*' Leah replied '*the teacher likes it to look like that.*'

There are two aspects to choosing an effective and efficient method of calculation. First the size and type of numbers involved. The fact that 1 999 and 2 001 are close together makes a 'counting on' strategy seem fairly obvious. What about if the numbers had been 1 876 and 2 034? Now the second aspect is rather more obvious: how confident the person doing the calculation is in their 'number sense'. One person may feel sufficiently at home with numbers to trust that they can mentally calculate what needs to be added to 1 876 to make it up to 2 034, but someone else may put more trust in a written method (or in using a calculator).

The 'traditional' methods for written long multiplication and long division calculations are probably familiar to you. Remember practice pages of calculations like:

$$\begin{array}{r} 345 \\ \times\ \ 27 \\ \hline \end{array} \qquad \text{or} \qquad 32\overline{\smash{)}2748}$$

But methods change and are not cast in stone. In the 1950s and 1960s most people were taught to do paper and pencil subtractions using 'equal additions' ('ten to the top and ten to the bottom'):

$$\begin{array}{r} 563 \\ -\ 257 \\ \hline \end{array}$$

You cannot subtract 7 from 3 so add ten to the top and ten to the bottom:

$$\begin{array}{r} 56\overset{1}{3} \\ -\ 2\underset{1}{5}7 \\ \hline 306 \end{array}$$

While equal additions is an effective method, it is not easy to explain why it works. In effect, the calculation you end up carrying out is actually 573 – 267 and knowing that this is going to give you the same answer is not immediately obvious.

So what are the key differences between written and mental methods?

	Mental	Written
Start with	**the numbers** In carrying out a mental method, the initial focus is on the numbers, as complete, whole numbers, in order to get a feel for the calculation	**the operation** In carrying out a written method the initial focus is likely to be on the operation – written methods imply set procedures for certain operations, the size and type of numbers are immaterial
Method depends on	**the numbers and relationship between them** So, for example, to find 205 – 198 a counting on strategy (it's 2 to 200 and another 5, that's 7) is appropriate but would be an inefficient method for 205 – 12, which is more likely to be a calculation by some form of counting back (five off leaves 200, another 7 off leaves 193).	**what method has been taught** If decomposition is the chosen method for subtraction then it makes no difference if the calculation is 205 – 198 or 205 – 12.
Calculation carried out	**may be transformed** In the example above, 205 – 198 is found by using an addition strategy, rather than by actually doing a subtraction.	**is the one specified** Since the method of calculation is all important, that takes priority.

International comparisons

An international survey of numeracy compared how well adults in seven countries, including the UK, performed on basic number tasks (Basic Skills Agency, 1997).

One question asked participants to multiply 6×21. Eighty-three per cent of the UK sample answered this correctly. The next question on the survey asked them to multiply 16×21. The success rate on this question for UK adults in the sample was only 60%.

The research report indicates that 17% of the UK sample either refused or indicated that they could not answer 16×21, compared to 8% for 6×21.

One possible reason for this reduction in the success rate is that the second question 'cued' the adults into being expected to use a written, long multiplication method, rather than strategically building on the previous answer.

Bugs

Daniel was working through a page of subtractions of tens and units, using the method of decomposition. Here is some of his working:

56	63	78	82
− 24	− 37	− 55	− 49
32	34	23	47

Why does Daniel get some correct and others wrong?

You may have noticed that Daniel's errors are not the result of carelessness or lack of knowing the number bonds to 10, but arise out of a 'bug' in his method. So why might he be making such an error? One possible explanation rests on children's early experience of number operations and the move into recording them.

When young children first meet arithmetic and begin to record additions they may not appreciate that 3 + 4 arises out of a different experience (take three things and add four to them) from 4 + 3 (take four things and add three to them). It is one of the neatnesses and strengths in mathematics that the answer to 3 + 4 turns out to be the same as that of 4 + 3. This commutative property of addition is put into good use – given 2 + 33, it is simpler to think of it as 33 + 2.

Young children interpret the form of recording differently. If they have four counters and three counters to add together then the 4 and the 3 are recorded with the + put between them to indicate what to do with the numbers – add them. With this understanding (and notice that it is a sensible way of using the symbols) recording 4 + 3 or 3 + 4 does not matter – each stands for the same.

It is only when subtraction is introduced that they may become aware of the need to record in a particular order. Having five objects and taking away two is recorded as either 5 − 2 or 2 − 5. As far as the child is concerned, each means 5 and 2 are the numbers to use and 'take away' in the operation. Since, to the five-year-old, it is clearly nonsense to try and take five away from two, and they do not appreciate the need to 'read' 2 − 5 in this way, from their point of view the recording is not problematic.

However, teacher, being aware of the difficulties in letting children record 2 − 5 = 3, may try to explain that the order of digits matters and encourage children to record it differently because 'you cannot take a larger number from a smaller one'. Later on, children like Daniel remember this rule and get into difficulty with vertical subtractions.

Rules – always true?

- Is it true that you cannot take a larger number from a smaller one?

- Can you think of other 'rules' that might be said to children, or perhaps that you were taught, that are not strictly mathematically correct?

- Sometimes children 'invent' rules for themselves without being told them explicitly. For example, when they first meet multiplication children always work with whole numbers and so deduce that 'multiplication always makes bigger'.

- What other 'false' rules might children invent for themselves?

We now have one possible explanation for Daniel's bug. His understanding of place value is not sufficiently strong for him to be able to 'repair' his method of subtraction.

The idea of bugs and repair comes from the work of Brown and Burton (1978). Work of others following on from this has suggested that children's errors in written calculations arise out of three sources:

- carelessness;

- lack of knowledge of number bonds;

- 'bugs' in procedures.

A book by Ashlock (1982) contains many examples of the sorts of bugs that children can develop, provided through samples of work to analyse.

Another bug

The example of Jo is typical of the sort of errors that pupils can make in learning standard algorithms. When adding two three-digit numbers, Jo would arrive at results like:

$$
\begin{array}{r}
375 \\
+\ 487 \\
\hline
1\ 3\ 12 \\
\scriptstyle 6\ \ 1
\end{array}
$$

When asked to explain her working, Jo would say: 'five and seven is twelve, put the two down and carry the one. Seven and eight and one is sixteen, put the one down and carry the six. Three and four and six is thirteen'. Asked why she put down the one and carried the six in the middle column, Jo would reply: 'Well, I'm in the tens column, there is one ten in sixteen, so I put the ten down and carry the six'.

Jo seems typical of many pupils who, having had a lot of experience of column arithmetic, ceases to treat the numbers in a holistic way, focusing instead on treating them as though they were single digits. As we saw in the chapter on mental methods, some people argue that part of the reason for this is a result of children being introduced to calculations in a vertical form before they need to be able to write them in this way. The sum 3 + 4 does not need to be set out vertically, because carrying out the calculation does not depend on having to deal with digits in a column-by-column way.

Even when pupils can carry out the algorithm correctly on paper this does not necessarily mean that misunderstandings about the process are not present.

Written smaller means getting smaller

The Children's Mathematical Frameworks (CMF) project (Hart, Johnson, Brown, Dickson, & Clarkson, 1989) gives examples of pupil' misunderstandings behind correct calculations. For example, one pupil in carrying out a subtraction by decomposition changed 307 to $\overset{2}{3}\overset{1}{0}7$. Asked if the number on the top of the sum was still 307 the pupil's responses show some confusion:

P: No.

I: No. What's it now then?

P: One thousand, ten hundred and seventeen.

I: Good gracious me, has it changed then?

P: Yes.

I: Well, has it got bigger, has it got smaller or is it just the same but in a different form?

P: It's got smaller.

In the same project, the researchers identified misconceptions such as a child who always put a 9 in a column each time he carried out a subtraction using decomposition, possibly arising from the fact that he had been told that 'a column cannot hold more than nine'. Other pupils spoke of moving tens into another place as the result of 'lack of space'. The researchers suggest that providing incomplete and simplified explanations may not only fail to help some children but actually confuse them.

Many people still think of the main purpose of primary mathematics as making sure that children are well versed in the four rules of arithmetic. All that children like Daniel need, they argue, is lots more practice. However, there is little evidence that more practice helps and as Brown and Burton (1978) have shown, children need to develop understanding as well as facility if they are to become effective at computations.

Until recently, the accepted wisdom on the teaching of written algorithms for addition and subtraction of two and three-digit numbers was through the use of structured practical apparatus. However, as pointed out in Chapter 2, research is beginning to show that the use of practical materials is not necessarily the most direct way of encouraging the move to paper and pencil.

There is some evidence that encouraging the pupils to make their own written recordings of what they did with the materials and then working with them to refine the records is more effective than expecting them to perform set routines with apparatus (Dickson, Brown and Gibson, 1984) .

However, the question remains: if pupils developed a more sound understanding of mental methods with two-digit numbers, would the practical experience be necessary at all? The commonly held belief that all mathematical experiences should be based in some sort of practical activity for 'real' understanding to occur may need to be reconsidered. Who displays more 'real' understanding, the pupil who can add 34 and 28 by reformulating this as 32 + 30 or the pupil who needs counting materials to find the answer?

There are two things in teaching children about paper and pencil methods that might lead to better understanding:

- incorporating children's own methods

    by challenging the children to find a way of calculating the answer using paper and pencil and then working with them to refine and 'tidy-up' their methods, leading to

- paper and pencil methods that are more 'transparent'

    that is, paper and pencil calculations where the method is clearer and easier to reconstruct if you forget it.

Teaching and learning paper and pencil methods for addition and subtraction

As discussed in Chapter 3, when working with children on adding two or three numbers mentally, the most effective strategy is to start with the 'most significant digits' first, that is the hundreds or tens. In dealing with addition, whenever possible children should be confident in finding the answer mentally. Certainly all children when they leave primary school might be expected to be able to mentally add or subtract any pair of two-digit numbers. Many can go beyond that and are confident to add mentally pairs of three-digit numbers (although they might want to jot the numbers down to help remember them).

However, there will be times when the numbers become difficult to handle mentally. This may be because the numbers are particularly large or because there is a string of numbers to total, for example, 45 + 5243 + 3 + 267 + 3189. Strings of numbers to total are a particularly good way to introduce children to paper and pencil methods of addition. If they can add 36 and 48 mentally then there is little point in expecting children to do this using paper and pencil. However, totalling 36 + 48 + 17 + 52 is rather more challenging. In such cases a paper and pencil method may be appropriate if electronic means of calculating are not available.

Given that the mental strategy is to start with the most significant digit first, it makes sense to introduce children to an extended form of paper and pencil calculating that builds on this mental strategy. For example, to add 549 and 386 the method would look like:

$$
\begin{array}{r}
549 \\
+\ 386 \\
\hline
800 \\
120 \\
15 \\
\hline
935
\end{array}
$$

Similarly, asked to total 45 + 5243 + 3 + 267 + 3189 the working would look something like:

$$
\begin{array}{r}
45 \\
5243 \\
3 \\
267 \\
+\ 3189 \\
\hline
8000 \\
500 \\
220 \\
27 \\
\hline
8747 \\
\end{array}
$$

Note that in each of these examples the calculation was initially presented in a horizontal format. If calculations are always presented to children in a horizontal format then they can choose whether or not to set them out as a vertical calculation or whether to find the answer using another method. For example, in totalling 45 + 5243 + 3 + 267 + 3189 a child might decide that it is sensible to rearrange the numbers somewhat, say by adding the 3 to the 267 and the 45 to the 5243 so the calculation becomes 5288 + 270 + 3189. Presenting the calculation already in a vertical format would discourage this and suggest to the children that there is only one acceptable method for finding the answer.

Rather than actually being taught any particular written method for addition and subtraction, children can be challenged to find a method. The teacher's task is then to help them refine their method.

Subtraction

A teacher of a Year 3 class challenged the children to see if they could find the answer to the following 'story'.

- Sally's best score on her computer game yesterday was 378. Her best score today was 525. How many more points did Sally score today?

The children were told that they could use whatever equipment they liked, but for that lesson, the teacher did not want them to use calculators. The children were asked to work in pairs and given about ten minutes to find the answer. During that time the teacher wandered around the class observing the different methods and deciding who she was going to invite to the front to example. In the end the teacher chose two pairs, Rashid and Amir, and Jenny and Kate.

Rashid and Amir explained that they had taken away the 300 first to leave 225. That left 78 to subtract. Then they had taken away 20 to leave 205, leaving 58 to subtract. They took away the 50 leaving 155 and then finally took away the 8 by taking off five, to leave 150 and then subtracting 3. The answer was 147.

As they explained, the teacher acted as a scribe jotting down their method:
525 − 300 => 225 − 20 => 205 − 50 => 155 − 5 => 150 − 3 => 147.

The teacher then showed the children how this method could be recorded vertically:

$$
\begin{array}{r}
525 \\
-\,378 \\
\hline
225 \\
205 \\
155 \\
150 \\
147 \\
\hline
\end{array}
$$

$$
\begin{array}{r}
-\,300 \\
-\;\;20 \\
-\;\;50 \\
-\;\;\;5 \\
-\;\;\;3 \\
\hline
378
\end{array}
$$

Jenny and Kate explained that they had used a 'counting on' method:
378 add 2 was 380, add 20 was 400, add 100 was 500, add 25 was 525. So 2 + 20 + 100 + 25 had been added on, a total of 147.

Again, the teacher scribed for the children:
378 + 2 => 380 + 20 => 400 + 100 => 500 + 25 => 525.
2 + 20 + 100 + 25 = 147

The teacher went on to show how this could also be recorded in a vertical form, keeping a running record of the numbers that had been added on.

$$
\begin{array}{r}
525 \\
-\,378
\end{array}
\qquad
\begin{array}{rr}
378 & \\
+\;\;\;2 & \qquad 2 \\
\hline
380 & \\
+\;\;20 & \qquad 22 \\
\hline
400 & \\
+\,100 & \qquad 122 \\
\hline
500 & \\
+\;\;25 & \qquad 147 \\
\hline
525 &
\end{array}
$$

The teacher worked through another example, using these two methods and then posed the children some similar problems to work on, either using one of these two methods or a method of their own.

Tradition in mathematics education

- How important is 'tradition' in mathematics teaching?

- How important is it that children set out their written calculations in a particular way?

- How could you convince parents that getting an answer with understanding is more important than how a calculation looks?

THINGS TO TRY

A new subtraction algorithm

Suppose you want to take 345 from 721.

Taking away from 999 is much easier so do that instead.

Add 721 to your answer.

Strike out the one at the front and add it to the total.

- Can you now do this for 468 from 813?

- Does it work for all numbers?

- Will you remember it in a week?

It would not be sensible for schools now to teach the above method for dealing with subtraction, but it does provide an interesting investigation for children at the upper end of Key Stage 2 to explore subtraction and to reason through why it works.

Teaching and learning about paper and pencil methods for multiplication and division

Again, children can learn and develop methods for long multiplication that are easier to understand and reconstruct if they forget the exact details.

Area model for long multiplication

One class of children had had a lot of experience working with the array model for multiplication. The teacher worked with the children in building their confidence for multiplying whole multiples of ten together, using diagrams like this:

$50 \times 40 =$

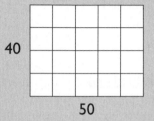

40

50

The teacher discussed with the children the area value of each small square in the diagram and everyone agreed that this was 100. As there were 20 squares in the diagram, they agreed the product was 20×100 or 2 000.

The teacher and the class went on to reduce the detail in the diagrams.

$50 \times 40 =$

40 $\quad$ 20 × 100

50

$50 \times 40 = 2\ 000$

The children went on to practise using this method until they were confident in multiplying whole multiples of ten together.

The teacher challenged the children to see if they could find a way to extend their diagram to be able to find the solution to $34 \times 27 =$. As the children worked on this, their teacher observed and listened to them carefully to choose one or two children to come to the front and share their methods. This led to the children being able to work with diagrams like this:

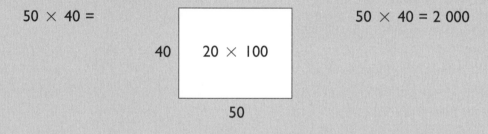

$34 \times 27 =$

$600 + 210 + 80 + 28 = 918$

From here it was a short step to the children feeling confident to miss out the diagram, but also having this image to fall back on if they were unsure about their workings.

$$53 \times 46$$

$50 \times 40 =$	2000
$50 \times 6 =$	300
$3 \times 40 =$	120
$3 \times 6 =$	18
	2438

The traditional paper and pencil algorithm for division is based on repeated subtraction, but the density of the layout masks this. Children can be introduced to other paper and pencil methods for division, based on repeated subtraction, again where the working behind the method is clearer.

For example, $186 \div 8$ (note again the horizontal presentation of the calculation to avoid suggesting a particular method).

$$
\begin{array}{rl}
186 & \\
-\ \ 80 & (8 \times 10) \\
\hline
106 & \\
-\ \ 80 & (8 \times 10) \\
\hline
26 & \\
-\ \ 24 & (8 \times 3) \\
\hline
2 & (10 + 10 + 3) \qquad \text{Answer 23 remainder 2}
\end{array}
$$

Again, $671 \div 24$

$$
\begin{array}{rl}
671 & \\
-\ 240 & (24 \times 10) \\
\hline
431 & \\
-\ 240 & (24 \times 10) \\
\hline
191 & \\
-\ 120 & (24 \times 5) \\
\hline
71 & \\
-\ \ 48 & (24 \times 2) \\
\hline
23 & (10 + 10 + 5 + 2) \quad \text{Answer 27 remainder 23 (or } 27\,^{23}/_{24}\text{)}
\end{array}
$$

ACTIVITY 1 *Calculating catalogue*

This case study is written with the focus of attention on addition and subtraction of two- or three-digit numbers. The activity is easily adapted for exploring multiplication and division. It is designed to help children develop flexible methods of calculation and has links with using and applying mathematics, as it requires the children to select the mathematics to use for a task and check the results.

Organisation

Although children could do this activity on their own, they will get more out of it if they have the opportunity to work in pairs and discuss their methods. Little preparation is required, other than to provide the children with large sheets of paper and coloured pens.

Starting off

Ask a child to write on the board a two- or three-digit number addition, for example 278 + 136. Ask the children to work in pairs to find the answer. As the children are working, make a mental note of who to ask to share their method with the rest of the children. Invite chosen pairs to come forward and explain how they found the answer. For example, someone might suggest adding 200 and 100 then 70 and 30 and 8 + 6, finally adding the three totals together. Another method might be to add 100 to 278 then add 70 and finally add 8. Try to gather at least three different methods.

Developing the activity

Ask the children to work in pairs and to make up a two- or three-digit subtraction calculation (for example, 542 – 365). Their task is to design a poster that will clearly show three different methods for doing the subtraction. Encourage them to try out their ideas in rough first and to think about how they will make their method clear to the other children.

Sharing outcomes

Display the posters and discuss with the children the different methods. How many methods did the children find altogether? Did any pair come up with a method that was completely different from all the others?

Questions to ask

- How do you decide which method is the 'best'?

- Which methods are easiest to follow?

- Which methods would work with any size of number?

Providing for differentiation

There are different types of differentiation that operate within this activity. First, the children are writing their own calculations to work on, so they are in some control over the level of difficulty here. You might want to direct some children to work specifically with two or three digits according to their level of attainment.

Second, there is differentiation by outcome according to the different methods that the children use.

ACTIVITY 1   *Calculating catalogue (Continued)*

Assessment opportunities

The whole of this activity provides plenty of opportunities for assessment. As the children are working independently, there is time for you to observe them as they go about the task. The final poster provides a product that contains useful assessment information from the methods shown.

Communication

The production of a poster requires the children to communicate their methods to others. Look out for whether the children explain their method in terms that apply only to the particular calculation, or do they show how their method could work for any numbers?

Progression

There are two aspects of progression that you can address. First, challenging the children to explore which of their methods would work effectively with larger numbers. Second, can they refine any of their methods to make them more efficient?

Consolidation

Children who need more support could be asked to make up five more calculations and use each of their methods to find the solution. Do they get the same answer each time? If not, can they sort out where they have gone wrong?

Links within the mathematics curriculum

The activity will encourage children to attend to the link between addition and subtraction.

Ask the children to produce a poster of three different story problems to go with a given calculation.

Links across the curriculum

Get the children to bring in advertisements clipped from magazines. What makes for a good advert? Can they design an advert to 'sell' one of their calculating methods?

ACTIVITY 2 *Broken calculator*

This case study activity requires the children to work with all four rules of number and is designed to help develop their understanding of the connections between the four rules. It links with using and applying in that it will require the children to find ways to overcome obstacles and check their results.

Organisation

The activity requires the children to work in pairs and each pair will need a calculator as well as paper and pencil.

Starting off

Explain to the pair of children that this activity has a particular 'ground-rule' that they must stick to:

■ each of the pairs takes a turn to operate the calculator and both must agree on what is to be punched into the calculator **before** either partner presses a key.

It is important to emphasise this ground rule to encourage the children to discuss what is going on and to discourage one of the pair simply taking over. You will probably have to remind the children of the ground rule while they are working on the activity.

Ask the children to imagine that the 6 button on the calculator is broken – nothing happens to the screen if you press it. Putting a sticky label over this button can help remind the children not to use it. Explain that although the button is broken, a 6 can still be shown on the calculator display. If the calculators have memories and the children know how to use these, also ask them not to use the memory.

Ask the pairs to decide how they could get 66 to show on the calculator display without using the 6 button. Emphasise that they need to decide which keys they are going to press **before** they press any of them. What different methods do the children come up with?

Developing the activity

Put up on the board a range of calculations, all of which involve some sixes, for the children to find the answers to. For example:

$$
\begin{array}{lll}
\begin{array}{r} 54 \\ \times\ 6 \end{array} & \begin{array}{r} 236 \\ -\ 69 \end{array} & \text{The difference} \\
 & & \text{between} \\
 & & \text{56 and 364} \\
 & & \qquad\qquad 256 \div 8 \\
62 \times 26 & 263 \div 62 & 48 + 26
\end{array}
$$

Children who finish all of your calculations should make up some similar ones for their friends to work out the answers to.

As the children work on the activity, encourage them to stick to the ground rule. You might want to note any particularly inventive methods that pairs come up with, and that you would want them to share with the rest of the class later.

ACTIVITY 2 *Broken calculator (Continued)*

Sharing outcomes

Get some of the children to explain to the others the different methods that they used to get round the broken 6.

Questions to ask

- Which was the easiest calculation to figure out?

- Which was the hardest?

- Did anybody try anything on the calculator the results of which surprised them?

Providing for differentiation

The fact that the children are having to find their own methods of overcoming the problem provides for differentiation by outcome. Asking the children to make up some more calculations provides further differentiation by task.

Assessment opportunities

By listening to and observing children as they work on the activity there is plenty of opportunity to assessing their understanding of the operations.

Communication

The 'discuss then press' ground rule is designed to encourage children to share their thinking. Explaining their methods to the others will require good communication skills.

Progression

Children who are doing well could be challenged with questions like, find 65% of 660. Children can be further challenged by having to imagine that the multiplication button is broken.

What would happen if a calculator only had the 6, +, and − buttons working.

Consolidation

Generally the problems are easier to overcome with addition and subtraction than with multiplication and division, so you might want to provide further addition and subtraction calculations for children who are struggling with multiplication and division.

Links within the mathematics curriculum

The whole of this activity requires children to be flexible in their choice of methods and operations and to develop their understanding of the links between the four operations.

Links across the curriculum

The activity could be used to link into a design and technology challenge: suppose you were going to design a calculator that only had four keys on it. What would you choose for the four keys?

ACTIVITY BANK FOR DEVELOPING UNDERSTANDING METHODS OF CALCULATING

All of the following activities are based on the same resource: a small collection of cards, each with a single numeral on them. Unless stated otherwise, the children need a set of four cards. The activities can be done with the children working individually, but working in pairs provides more opportunity for discussion.

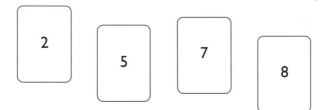

Shuffle them

Give pairs or individuals a set of four different digit cards. Ask the children to turn the cards over and mix them up. They turn over two cards and add the numbers together. Turn over the other two and add the two numbers. Now ask the children to add the two totals. Turn the cards over and repeat again. What do the children notice? Why is the total always the same?

Layout

Arrange the cards to form a two by two square. Find the total for each row and each column.

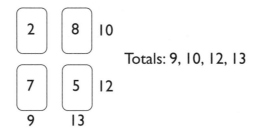

Totals: 9, 10, 12, 13

If the cards are rearranged, are different totals possible? (There are six different totals that can be made.)

Extend the activity to six cards laid out in a two by three array.

Two-digit total

Lay out the cards in pairs and 'read' them as two two-digit numbers. Add the two numbers. How many different totals can be made. Can the children put them in order?

$$2\ 8\ +\ 7\ 5\ =\ 103$$

ACTIVITY BANK FOR DEVELOPING UNDERSTANDING METHODS OF CALCULATING (Continued)

String total

Provide some cards with addition symbols on them. Lay out the four cards in a row with addition symbols inserted at different places. How many different totals can be created? What is the largest

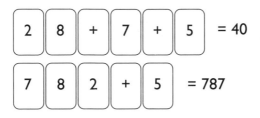

possible total? What is the smallest possible?

One to ten

Provide some cards with the symbols for all four operations and some cards with brackets on. Can

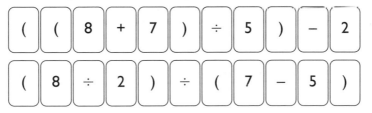

the children arrange the cards so as to create calculations that have answers from 1 to 10? One to 20? One to 100?

Three digits

How many three-digit numbers can be made with the cards? Put them in order from the smallest to the largest. What is the total of all the numbers?

Suppose there had been five cards. How many different three-digit numbers could be made then? Six cards? Can the children predict how many different three-digit numbers could be made from nine different cards?

Target numbers

Provide a list of target numbers to create, using some or all of the digits. For example: the largest even number, the odd number closest to 1 000, a multiple of 5, a multiple of 3 and 5, the smallest number greater than 200 and so on.

Pyramids

Lay the cards out in a row. Form three totals by adding pairs of adjacent cards and writing the total above. Add the three totals in pairs to form two new totals, and write these above. Finally, add these two totals to find the grand total.

ACTIVITY BANK FOR DEVELOPING UNDERSTANDING METHODS OF CALCULATING (Continued)

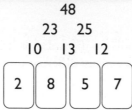

What happens to the grand total if you change the order of the cards?

Use the five digits from 1 to 5. Can they be arranged so that the grand total can be any number from 50 to 59?

Two-digit product

Lay out the cards in pairs and 'read' them as two two-digit numbers. Multiply the two numbers. How many different products can be made?

$$\boxed{2}\,\boxed{8} \times \boxed{7}\,\boxed{5} = 2\,100$$

Greatest product

Arrange the cards to make two numbers, either two two-digit numbers or a three-digit number and a single-digit number. Multiply the two numbers together. What is the largest possible answer?

$$\boxed{2}\,\boxed{8}\,\boxed{7} \times \boxed{5} = 1\,435$$

6

SOLVING NUMERICAL PROBLEMS

Introduction

Some Year 4 children were given paper with empty boxes on it and asked to imagine that these were blank calculator keys. Their teacher read out to them some 'story' problems and asked them not to find the answer but to fill in the boxes with the keys that they would press on the calculator to find the answer.

For example, the children were asked which set of calculator keys they would press to find the answer to:

■ John has 26 marbles. He wins 18 more. How many marbles does he now have?

Most of the children realised that the operation to use here was addition and filled in the boxes correctly:

However, what to put in the boxes was less straightforward when the children were given problems like the following:

■ Jane has 23 sweets and Jo has 15. How many more sweets has Jane got?

Many of the children put this in the boxes:

They had to work the answer out mentally, and what they thought they could put into the calculator required them to know the answer. The children were then given this problem:

■ Sanjit has 1 789 stamps in his album and Rashid has 2 456 stamps. How many more stamps does Rashid have?

These same children wrote down that you cannot do this on a calculator!

As this example illustrates, being able to solve a numerical problem means more than simply being able to 'spot' which calculation to use to reach an answer. Children need to learn to 'make sense' of problems. In order to help them to do this, they need to have experience of applying the four rules of arithmetic to a variety of situations.

Solving problems can also help children make sense of the different operations. They can come to appreciate that there is not necessarily one correct method for arriving at a solution and that there are links between the different operations. For example, working on a problem where one child uses repeated addition and another uses multiplication can provide a focus of discussion on the relative merits of each and help children realise that being flexible can be useful.

Children also need to develop ways of making sense of solutions. Through solving problems, as opposed to simply carrying out calculations, children can be helped to realise that getting the answer is not sufficient on its own. Answers must be made sense of within the context that gave rise to the calculation. Asked 'how many coaches each holding 25 people are required to take 60 children to the park?', many children will give the answer 2 remainder 10. The child who engages with the context and tries to make sense of the mathematics will realise that the sensible answer is 3 coaches. Often school mathematics does not encourage such insight as the focus is primarily just on doing calculations.

This chapter examines these different aspects of making sense of numerical problems.

National Curriculum expectations

The Programme of Study at Key Stage 1 expects that children should understand different aspects of addition and subtraction, for example taking away and finding differences and to understand that addition and subtraction are not totally separate operations but are related. Children should be able to apply them to various situations that involve whole numbers, including money problems.

Similarly Key Stage 1 children are also expected to understand different aspects of multiplication and division, for example sharing and repeated subtraction as instances of division. Again, they should be able to use them to solve problems with whole numbers (including money) and where necessary handle remainders appropriately.

In solving numerical problems, Key Stage 1 children should be able to choose a suitable method of computation, using apparatus or a calculator for large numbers and begin to check answers and have a feel for whether an answer is of an appropriate size.

The Programme of Study at Key Stage 2 expects that children should develop these understandings to use all four operations to solve problems, with a calculator if appropriate and including problems on money and measures.

Such problems may require several steps in their solution and Key Stage 2 children are expected to be able to choose, adapt and accurately apply sequences of methods of computation. As in Key Stage 1 they are also expected to check results using different methods (for example repeating operations in a different order) and have a sense of appropriate answers through estimation and approximation.

Teaching and learning about solving numerical problems

Traditionally, solving problems using the four operations was simply another set of arithmetical calculations, wrapped up in words. The problems on multiplication came at the end of the chapter on multiplication, so it did not take much effort to work out which calculation to use.

Many school texts continue to present a narrow view of what is meant by problem solving. 'Problems' are usually just calculation exercises wrapped up in words.

■ Five rabbits were by the side of the road. Three moved away. How many were left?

A distinction can be made between 'realistic' problems and 'routine' problems. The former are situations, problems and questions that might actually arise in the world. For example, 51 biscuits have been baked for the fair. If six biscuits are to be put into each bag, how many bags will be used?

Routine problems in contrast tend to be contrived situations that are created with the primary purpose of having to carry out a particular calculation or procedure: Mary bakes 28 strawberry and blackcurrant jam tarts. $\frac{3}{7}$ are strawberry. How many are blackcurrant?

In contrast to 'realistic' problems, 'routine' problems are unlikely ever to be encountered anywhere other than in mathematics lessons.

One other sort of non-routine problem that is worth considering is the 'curious' problems. These are problems that have little practical application but capture children's interest because of their curiosity value. For example:

■ If all the children in the school lay down, head to toe, would they stretch as far as a mile?

■ If you could have your weight in pound coins, how much would you be worth?

To encourage the children to engage with situations and try and make sense of them we need to present them with realistic and curious problems.

Routine word problems	Realistic/curious problems
What to find is clear	What to find may not be obvious
Only the exact information needed to find the answer is provided	Too much or too little information may be provided
One correct method is expected	Many methods may be possible
There is one correct answer	There may be a number of answers or even no answer
The answer can be found quickly	May require time and perseverance.

(adapted from Baroody, 1993)

Children need experience of non-routine realistic or curious problems, **in a variety of contexts,** in order to develop their mathematical thinking skills.

Children whose experience is limited to routine problems come to learn that the context of the problem is not particularly relevant. Children come to treat the context as 'window dressing' and ignore it. Instead they choose an operation on the size and type of numbers involved. In an American study 95% of 9-year-olds assessed gave an answer of 62 to the following:

■ There are 34 sheep and 28 goats on a ship How old is the captain?

Another non-mathematical strategy that pupils develop to help them deal with word problems is to try and spot 'key' words in the problem that will enable them to 'spot' which operation to use. For example, a pupil may decide that 'more' is associated with addition: Jim has five marbles and he wins three more. How many does he have now? But there is no simple one-to-one match between words and operations. Consider the different senses of more than in each of these questions.

■ Jane has eight marbles more than Jo. Jo has five marbles. How many marbles does Jane have?

■ Jane has eight marbles. Jo has five marbles. How many marbles more than Jo does Jane have?

Another popular trick is to decide which operation to use on the basis of the size of the numbers in the 'problem'. Small numbers must be multiplied, large ones added or divided.

Ruth

Fielker (1978) gives the example of a girl, Ruth, who had done a card of 'word' problems and asked him to mark them. The answers were all correct and the girl asked why one of the problems was a 'times'. Since she had correctly interpreted the problem as a multiplication Fielker asked her to explain to him how she had known it was a 'times'. Ruth explained that she knew that particular card had hard problems on it and since the numbers in that particular question were 5 and 6, adding or subtracting would have been too easy, so she had multiplied the numbers.

Behaviourist learning theories suggest that because this technique of spotting the key word sometimes does work, the pupils are provided with an intermittent reward system and strongly reinforced in their use of this approach. In fact, some teachers even encourage it!

There is a growing body of research evidence that suggests such tricks only enable pupils to succeed at school mathematics. They do not generalise to other situations and do not help pupils develop mathematical thinking. Even slight changes to the wording of problems confuse the pupils and being able to apply mathematics to real life situations where the problem is not clearly defined is almost impossible for many pupils. All the pupils learn is that mathematics is a series of tricks, not something that requires effort and thought but is ultimately very useful.

Realistic and curious problems need to be initially selected to be at a level that is challenging to the children, but not too threatening. Another change of emphasis that needs to be conveyed is that situations presented are not to be treated as 'spot the sum'. Working on non-routine problems is not one of: you have learnt your number bonds to ten in the abstract and now you need to learn to apply them. Rather, it is in the spirit of the fact that struggling to get to grips with how to solve a situation leads to deeper understanding of the mathematics.

In discussing the problems with the children it is important to focus on the methods they used, rather than whether or not they got the right answer. Exploring the methods that lead up to wrong answers can be just as fruitful as exploring correct methods, if not more so.

Which comes first – problems or methods?

One model of the problem solving process looks like this:

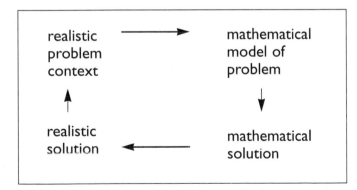

The child is presented with a realistic problem and has to find or create a mathematical model of the problem. Having found a solution to the mathematical problem this has to be re-interpreted as a realistic solution.

A popular belief in teaching mathematics is that children need to learn the 'right-hand side' part of this diagram first. They need to learn mathematical skill and procedures – how to add or multiply for example – before they can learn to use these skills or procedures in a problem-solving situation. Problems are used as a way of **applying** already learnt mathematical skills.

The 'traditional' approach is then to take a particular arithmetical skill/number bond and 'wrap' it up in different contexts. So number bonds to ten would involve marbles, cakes, children and so on, all in different situations – the idea being that the abstract number is 'extracted' from the situations, and also that because of the range of contexts presented, pupils somehow come to realise that the mathematics can be applied to lots of contexts. Unfortunately research is beginning to show that this does not happen!

An alternative model, as we discussed in Chapter 5, is to take 'realistic' situations and explore all the different ways that mathematics might arise – one situation leading to lots of mathematics (as opposed to one piece of mathematics leading to lots of situations).

So rather than having a particular mathematical model in mind when presenting children with realistic problems, they should be encouraged to use any of the different ways of working to solve the problem. For example, there is a world of difference between being given a situation like:

■ Chris got five birthday cards from friends and six from family. How many cards did Chris get?

and being given counters, possibly shown how to set up the model and then being left to practise similar 'problems'

and discussing the situation:

■ Chris bought a packet of 25 postcards, sent seven to friends and gave away three

and discussing what the problem is, how it might be solved, how you could check, and then sending a group away to find a solution and come back with some representation to share with the group.

However, it is clear that if the problem situation is one that is familiar and makes sense to the children then they can be motivated to find a solution. Their method may not be very sophisticated and not terribly efficient, so the role of the teacher is to help the children refine their solution method. Problems are used as a way of **learning** new mathematical skills.

This way of working really requires the situations to be introduced verbally – another reason why they have to present some challenge to the pupils – otherwise they complete them too quickly!

The main teaching that takes place happens **after** the solution has been found (again a reversal of the traditional model) – the sharing of the different methods and representations, the discussion about the advantages of particular methods, the possible feeding in of new methods – not in the sense of 'your methods were wrong' but in the sense of ' let me share with you how I would do it'. Further problems can be generated by asking children to make up similar problems for their friends to work on.

Problems of sense and problems of scale

Lave (1992) suggests that are actually two types of problem solving situations: *problems of sense* and *problems of scale.*

Problems of sense are ones where the context of the problem is important and needs to be taken into account in order to set up an appropriate mathematical model and interpret the solution. For example, in planning a picnic for a Year 1 class, the children had to figure out how much bread to buy in the context of how much they estimated everyone would eat. When someone made a slip up and got an answer that suggested they would need to buy 65 loaves of bread, the children knew this could not be right, as the context made sense and helped them. There would be more than two loaves per child, which was clearly impossible.

In problems of sense the solution has to be checked against the context in order to give a reasonable answer.

Problems of scale are problems where the mathematics has to be 'trusted' and relied upon as the context may not help provide either a sense of how to solve the problem or the reasonableness of the answer, because the scale of the problem makes the context difficult to grasp. Examples of problems of scale would include: How much water do you use in a day? Have you lived a million hours?

In finding solutions to problems of scale, the methods of calculation need to be carefully attended to and checked. The reasonableness of the answer cannot be decided simply on the context of the problem.

Lave argues that much of the difficulty that pupils display arises from treating problems of sense as though they were problems of scale. That is, relying heavily on the mathematics to the exclusion of the context.

In posing realistic or curious problems for children to work on, it is helpful to think about three different 'unknowns' that can need to be found (see Fuson, 1992):

1) **Start unknown:** the initial quantity needs to be found

- Jo bakes some currant buns. After we had eaten three there were nine left. How many did Jo bake?
  (❏ – 3 = 9, possibly calculated as 9 + 3 = ❏)

- Mrs Green put some apples into bags. She ended up with six bags of apples, each containing five apples. How many apples did she start with?
  (❏ ÷ 5 – 6, possibly calculated as 5 × 6 = ❏)

2) **Change unknown:** the second quantity has to be found

- Jo baked 20 currant buns. Someone sneaked down in the night and ate some. The next morning Jo found there were only 15 in the tin. How many were eaten?
  (20 – ❏ = 15, possibly calculated as 15 + ❏ = 20)

- Mrs Green picked 24 pears. She put them in bags for the school fête. When she had finished she had eight bags each with the same number of pears in them. How many pears were in each bag?
  ($8 \times \square = 24$ or $24 \div \square = 8$)

3) **Result unknown:** the final quantity has to be found

- Jo baked 12 lemon buns and 12 cherry buns. How many buns were there altogether?
  ($12 + 12 = \square$)

- Mrs Green had 36 peaches. She put four into each bag. How many bags did she fill?
  ($36 \div 4 = \square$)

Word problems like this, when presented in text books, tend to concentrate on problems where the result is unknown. As the examples above show, setting problems where the start or change is unknown provide more opportunity for children to discuss alternative mathematical models for solving the problem.

As a further refinement to the above three-way classification, addition and subtraction situations can be classified into four types:

1) **Join** problems involve the action of adding elements to a given set.

- Walking through the park in Autumn I picked up five leaves, then I found another seven that had different colours on them. How many leaves did I take to school?
  ($5 + 7 = \square$)

2) **Separate** problems involve the action of removing items.

- My teacher asked us to take some leaves in for the nature table. I collected 15. On the way to school I met my friend who had forgotten to collect any leaves, so I gave her four. How many leaves did I take into school?
  ($15 - 4 = \square$)

3) **Part-part-whole** problems involve comparisons within a set.

- My group had 40 leaves on the table. We had to sort our from our leaves the ones that we thought were mostly brown. We decided that 12 leaves were mostly brown. How many were in the other set?
  ($40 - 12 = \square$, or $12 + \square = 40$)

4) **Compare** problems involve comparisons between two sets.

- My teacher asked me to work with a partner and to look at each other's leaves. My partner had collected 25 leaves and I had taken in 17. How many more leaves did my partner have?
  ($25 - 17 = \square$ or $17 + \square = 25$)

Join and separate problems are easier for children to solve. The 'action' that is contained in the context of the story helps them make sense of which mathematical operation to use. Because nothing is added to or removed from the situation, part-part-whole and compare problems are harder for children to understand. How can this be a 'take-away' when nothing has been taken away.

Difficulties in solving problems

In the 1994 National Tests for mathematics, seven-year-old children were asked

- 56 × 100 =

and

- Sam has 50p. Chris has 10 times as much. How much has Chris got?

In a way, both of these questions are assessing whether children can multiply by a power of 10. The test results showed that children had difficulties in both questions, but fewer were able to answer the second question, even though the calculation is simpler (SCAA, 1994).

The Assessment of Performance Unit presented 11-year-olds with two items requiring them to calculate 4 × 37 and 9 × 37 in the context of money:

- Tariq's cat is called Sammy. Sammy eats four tins of cat food each week. Each tin costs 37p. How much does Tariq spend on cat food for Sammy each week?

- Josephine's dog is called Reggie. Reggie eats nine tins of dog food each week. Each tin costs 37p. How much does Josephine spend on dog food for Reggie each week?

The success rate on the first question was 52% but this dropped to 39% on the second question (Foxman *et al.*, 1991).

By providing children with examples of each type of problem and discussing them with the children, the relationship between the 'realistic' situation and the 'mathematical model' can be explored.

These examples illustrate that it is not simply the case that children find questions easier whether they are in or out of context. Children's familiarity of the context will affect their interpretation of the problem.

This suggests that teaching and assessing 'realistic' problems means providing pupils with:

- variety in the range of contexts that problems are set in;
- different levels of difficulty within the context in order.

The context can also exert an effect in terms of pupils interpreting their solutions. There are many examples in the literature of pupils giving answers which are nonsensical in the context of the problem.

Helping children solve numerical problems includes helping children decide on:

- what is the problem?
- which method of calculation?
- what might be a sensible solution?

What is the problem?

This is often the most difficult part. It is important that the children are helped to 'get inside' the situation to help them make the problem theirs. Ways to encourage this include:

- acting out the situation, getting the children to role play;

- modelling the situation, using practical materials to stand for the items in the problem;

- asking children to explain in their own words what they think the problem is about.

Rather than the teacher judging these explanations, encourage the children to listen carefully to each other and discuss whether they agree on the various interpretations. Asking the children to work in pairs is useful here.

Method of calculation?

Once the children have a sense of what the problem is about they need to make some decisions about how to go about solving it. This may include choosing between:

- which of the four rules seems most appropriate;

- whether to use a standard 'algorithm', a non-standard algorithm or an invented method;

- working mentally, with a calculator, using practical materials or paper and pencil.

Strategies for helping them do this include:

- setting them off to work on the problem for a short period of only about five minutes, then bringing the group or class together to discuss how different children have started;

- getting the children to work in pairs for a few minutes and then putting pairs together to share their working.

Sensible solution?

What is the answer to $13 \div 4 = \Box$?

Is it 3, 3 remainder 1, 3 and one-quarter or 3.25? Of course the answer is 'it all depends'. Three and three-quarters might be a sensible answer to sharing out 13 sausages between four people, but is not a reasonable answer to sharing out marbles! In some circumstances, four is the most sensible answer: try ordering 3.25 taxis each holding four people for party of 13.

Typical is a question from the Key Stage 2 1995 national tests where pupils were asked how many adults needed to accompany a school party of 427 children if one adult accompanies each group of 15 children.

Only a small proportion of pupils gave the correct answer of 29. Many gave an answer of 28. Others gave answers of 28.4666667 by doing the correct operation on a calculator but failing to interpret the answer in the context of the problem. Some did the division using paper and pencil but again failed to interpret the remainder correctly. Children need the opportunity to discuss their solutions in the light of the problem context (SCAA, 1995).

ACTIVITY 1 _Picnic_

This activity is an example of a realistic problem of sense for children to solve. The context is one which they may be reasonably familiar with and judgements about the method of solution and appropriate answers will be based on this sense making. The mathematical content concerns solving calculations involving money and estimation and approximation. With respect to 'using and applying' mathematics, this situation requires the children to make decisions.

Organisation

The activity requires very little advance preparation. The children may benefit from working on large sheets of paper.

Starting off

Discuss with the children the idea of going on a picnic. Brainstorm what they like to eat on a picnic by asking for suggestions and writing these up on the board. Work with the children on deciding some realistic prices for items that they would like to buy for a picnic. Record these against the names of the items.

Developing the activity

Ask the children to work together in groups of about four and to imagine that they are going on a picnic together. Give each group an amount to spend, chosen on the basis of their levels of understanding. So one group might have £4 to spend while another might have £6.

Set the groups off to plan their picnic within the cost allocated. They do not have to stick to the items suggested in the first part of the activity, but they should try and agree on realistic prices for other items that they decide to take.

Sharing outcomes

Invite the groups to report back on their different suggestions. As well as reporting back on the different decisions that they made, encourage the children to explain the methods that they used for calculating the various costs and the running total of money spent. Can they suggest ways to check their costs?

Which group do the children think managed to produce the most varied and imaginative picnic?

Questions to ask

- How much have you spent so far?
- How else could you work out that total?
- How did you decide on that price?

Providing for differentiation

The open-ended nature of the method of solving the problem allows opportunity for differentiation by outcome. As the groups can be set different starting amounts there is also the potential for differentiation by task.

ACTIVITY 1   *Picnic (Continued)*

Assessment opportunities

As the task is easily set up and explained, you should not have to spend too much time sorting out with the children what it is they have to do. This provides plenty of time for you to observe how the children are going about the calculations. You may want to make a note of any interesting methods that you will invite children to share with others. For example, a child or group might be using a long-winded way of doing a calculation and you want to get them to explain to the rest of the class so that the other children can help them refine their method. Alternatively, you may spot a child using an effective checking strategy that they could share with the others.

Communication

As the children have to share their ideas and work together as a group, the activity provides them with the opportunity to share and communicate their ideas in small groups. Presenting their solutions to the whole class gives them further experience of having to talk about the mathematics involved.

Progression

Children who are coping with the problem can be extended by adding in extra factors – more children going on the picnic, more refined prices, additional money.

Further challenges could include having to work out how much money it costs to feed a child for a week or deciding how many days could they feed themselves for on £5.

Consolidation

Children who are experiencing difficulty with the activity may find it easier to work on planning a packed lunch for one person. Providing them with coins (preferably real rather than plastic) will also help support them.

Links within the mathematics curriculum

This links in with general work on money. Links can also be made with measures by including items that cannot be bought in discrete quantities, for example cheese or grapes.

Links across the curriculum

Links could be made with a topic on food and healthy eating.
This activity and the following one are adapted from Askew and Ebbutt, 1997.

ACTIVITY 2   *A million-second holiday*

This is an example of a curious problem of scale that might engage the children's interest. It requires them to carefully reason through the mathematical calculations to check if their answers are sensible, rather than being able to rely on 'common sense' for the answers. The activity links with the number curriculum through using calculators to explore number structure and extending understanding of large numbers. Links with using and applying mathematics include having to decide on an appropriate sequence of computation to solve the problem and considering if there are better methods.

Organisation

Children will need access to paper and pencil and calculators, but that aside, little advance preparation is required.

Starting off

Discuss with the children the idea of a million seconds. Suppose they were to be given a holiday that would last a million seconds. What might they be able to do: have a day trip away, a weekend in Paris, a month in America, a year in Australia. Never have to work?

Ask the children to note down individually their estimates of how long a million-second holiday would last, for later reference.

Developing the activity

Encourage the children to work in pairs or small groups and to spend a few minutes discussing how they are going to work out how long a million seconds is. Ask the pairs or groups to note down the method that they think they are going to use to find out how long a million seconds is. Emphasise that they are not actually working it out at this point, just planning.

As the children are planning, listen to their ideas and make a note of one or two groups that you are going to invite to explain their method to the rest of the class.

Once the children have shared their methods and you have discussed the strengths and weaknesses of various ideas, set the groups off to work out how long they think a million seconds will be. Again, as the children are doing the working out, observe, listen and note what they are doing in order to focus the sharing of outcomes.

Sharing outcomes

How close are the different answers that the children have arrived at? (It is unlikely that they all reach exactly the same answer.) What are the longest and shortest times that have been calculated? Get the groups who came up with these to share their different methods. Do the rest of the children agree that the methods of calculation are accurate?

Discuss with the children the accuracy of their original estimations. Did anyone get close to the answer arrived at when calculating? How did they manage to do that? Did they make some sort of rough calculation or was it just a lucky guess?

ACTIVITY 2   *A million-second holiday (Continued)*

Questions to ask

- How many seconds in a day?

- Could you check that calculation in a different way?

- Suppose you were only given a thousand seconds, how would you work that out?

Providing for differentiation

The task is based around differentiation by outcome. Although children may vary in their understanding of what a million is, the task itself is easy enough to understand for them to be able to engage with it and find methods of solution.

Assessment opportunities

As the task is clear in terms of what the children have to do, you are free to encourage the children to explain what they are doing and so gain insight into their understandings.

In particular you might look out for children checking their results using a different method.

Communication

Checking that the answers arrived at are sensible ones encourages the children to present their results as clearly as possible, both orally and on paper.

Progression

It is unlikely that the children will all get exactly the same answer as different methods will lead to a certain amount of error. Discuss the differences with the children exploring how big a range of answers might be acceptable. They could also go on to look at different quantities. How long would a billion seconds be – a million, million? How long would a million days be?

Consolidation

Children are likely to approach the problem in one of two ways: either building up to a million seconds (number of seconds in a minute, then an hour, a day and then calculating a million's worth) or working down from a million (dividing by 60 to find out how many minutes, then by 60 for hours and so on). The former is probably slightly easier and might be the best way for less confident pupils to start.

Children who are having difficulty might be posed a simpler problem, for example, suppose you were given 100 hours' holiday. How long would that be?

Links within the mathematics curriculum

Reading, writing and ordering large numbers.

Children who are capable of it could work out the range of the answers and find the mean and mode of the different results arrived at.

Links across the curriculum

Link to topics on holidays, transport or time.

Contexts for realistic problems

School spending

Invite the children to think about the different things that schools have to buy each year: paper, pencils, paint and so on.

- How much does their class spend in a year on, say, paper?

- How much does the school spend in a year on, say, pencils?

School day

- How could you improve the school dinner times?

- What could be done to make wet playtimes better?

School tuck shop

Provide the children with a list of prices of items for sale. For example:

Crisps	20p
Apple	10p
Milk	12p
Juice	15p

Pose various questions to find the answer to. For example:

- Sheila has 30p to spend. What could she buy?

- Dylan buys a juice and an apple. How much change would he get from 40p?

- You have £10 to spend on an end of term 'feast' for the class. What would you buy from the tuck shop?

Invite the children to make up their own challenges.

Best buys

Ask the children to bring to school their favourite comics. Which do they think is the best buy? How will they define 'best'. What will they measure?

Decorating

How much would it cost to repaint the classroom? You will need to supply the children with costs of tins of paint.

ACTIVITY BANK FOR NUMERICAL PROBLEMS (Continued)

School concert

Provide the children with a list of information about an imaginary school concert.
For example:

- The hall can seat 120 people.

- Tickets cost £1.50 each for adults.

- Tickets cost 75p for children.

- Programmes are sold for 50p each.

- It cost £20 to photocopy the programmes.

- The concert lasts 1 hour and 45 minutes.

Pose a series of realistic problems for the children to solve using this information. For example:

- Seventy-five tickets have been sold. How many are still for sale?

- Jill sells 18 programmes. How much money is that?

- What time will the concert end?

- Shahid wants to come with his wife and three children. How much will the tickets cost?

Invite the children to make up further questions for them to swap with their friends.

What's the question?

This reverses the procedure – children are given the arithmetical calculation and have to write a question to go with it. Start off by providing a simple calculation, say 12 − 4. Check that the children can find the answer. Invite individual children to invent a realistic story problem to go with this calculation. For example, 'I picked 12 apples off the tree but four were rotten. How many could be eaten?'

Then give pairs of children different sets of 'linked' calculations, for example

15 + 3, 3 + 15, 18 ÷ 3, 18 ÷ 6.

Get them to work in pairs and make up several stories to accompany each calculation. Swap stories between pairs so they can work out the answers to each others' problems.

Contexts for curious problems

Letter sale

- Suppose you had to buy letters of the alphabet: £1 for A; £2 for B and so on up to £26 for Z. How much would your name cost?

ACTIVITY BANK FOR NUMERICAL PROBLEMS (Continued)

- Suppose you have £10 to spend on letters. What is the longest word you could 'buy'?
- What if the costs were reversed: £26 for A down to £1 for Z.
- Can the children find a book that they think contains close to 1 000 words. How could they check without counting every word?

Buttons

- How many buttons do the children think there are in total in the classroom? How will they find out?

Name lengths

- Who has the longest name in the class? Who has the shortest name? Have they included middle names?

Name snakes

Cut out strips of large squared paper 36 squares long. How many times can the children fit their first name on the strip, writing one letter in each square. Does anybody's name fit an exact number of times on the strip? What other words would fit on an exact number of times. What if the strip was 40 squares long?

Families and friends

How many people do the children estimate that they are related to? They could work on drawing up family trees and looking at how the pattern of numbers develops.

Suppose all their family and friends were going on a trip to the seaside. How many coaches would they need to hire?

I'd rather ...

Present the children with pairs of options related to individual and group statistics. For example, would you rather have

- your height as a stack of pound coins or your weight in 20p coins?
- a penny for every day that you have been alive or the same number of pounds as there are children in the school?

Long distance cycle

Suppose it were possible to cycle to the moon. How long would it take? The children will have to gather some practical information on cycling speeds, together with some text book information on the distance of the moon from the Earth.

7

SHAPE, SPACE AND MEASURES

Introduction

Too often one of the fundamental areas of mathematics – shape – is neglected because so much emphasis is placed on numeracy. So much so that many areas of shape are taught inadequately and children are often left with misconceptions about many aspects of the topic. There is also a disagreement about whether 2-dimensional shapes ought to be explored before 3-dimensional shapes. If we start from the child's view of the world then we perhaps ought to think about the fact that they live and play in a 3-dimensional environment and their exposure to 2 dimensions is limited and accessed only through books. For this reason I will explore the development of geometrical understanding starting from a 3-dimensional perspective.

Much of primary mathematics is concerned with discrete, countable quantities: numbers of children, spots on dice, beans in the jar. However, much of what we encounter in our everyday lives is continuous: time to program the video, ingredients for a cake, distance travelled. No continuous quantities can be 'counted' – given a bottle of water it makes no sense to say 'how many water is there?' One plus one equals one if you pour one cup of water into another. Measuring is the means by which continuous quantities are compared with discrete quantities and so become amenable to arithmetic. One litre of water plus one litre of water makes two litres of water.

Shape, space and measures then are concerned with how the world can be seen in a mathematical fashion. This chapter looks at ways of helping children put on such mathematical 'goggles'.

National Curriculum expectations

The shape and space content areas are divided into two aspects: shape and position and movement with developments in the level of complexity from Key Stage 1 to Key Stage 2. Understanding and using patterns and properties of shape involves work with 2-dimensional and 3-dimensional shapes and models, classifying properties and making use of the geometrical features including symmetry. Understanding and using properties of position and movement includes work on angles and transformations. Co-ordinates and tessellations feature at Key Stage 2.

Teaching and learning about shape and space

Children need to be given opportunities to develop an understanding of geometrical properties and relationships in order to solve a range of problems. They will also be expected to gain experience of pattern and transformations and to develop their understanding through practical work and with computers. The opportunity to draw on the mathematics of other cultures is encouraged.

Children bring to school many experiences of working with shapes. They will have probably played with balls, bricks, Lego and Duplo, post-it boxes, railway tracks, wheels, coins, cards. Experiences will also vary depending very much on whether they are a boy or a girl and their cultural and social background. The range of experience will be very diverse. Building on these early experiences of shape is important in establishing children's concepts of shape, and will often start from their own familiar experience.

van Hiele levels

Defining the possible development of geometrical understanding can be looked at through the levels described by Pierre and Dina van Hiele (1986). There are five van Hiele terms of which the first three or four are appropriate to Key Stages 1 and 2 of the mathematics national curriculum. Van Hiele Level 0 focuses on a process of visualisation in which children look at and describe a shape without considering the individual properties that combine to make that shape. For example, a cuboid is a 'box' and a rectangle is 'like a window' and the parts that make it look like that are not distinguished but rather the children refer to some object they are familiar with.

At van Hiele Level 1 children start to distinguish the components and the attributes of the shape. At this level children are able to distinguish the difference between one triangle and another and to articulate the properties of these shapes. For example, they can distinguish between a right-angled triangle and an equilateral triangle and explain simply why these distinctions can be made. This is known as the 'analysis stage'.

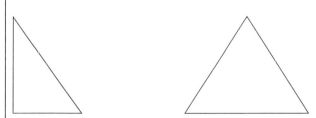

At Level 3, known as 'informal deductions', children can give the properties of shape that will define it uniquely as that shape. So an equilateral triangle will be defined as having three equal sides and three equal angles, the angles will each be 60°, that the angles will add up to 180°, and so on.

Reaching van Hiele Level 4, known as 'formal deduction', will enable a child to select sufficient conditions to uniquely define a shape. So in the case above they will know that an equilateral triangle can be determined by saying all its sides are equal or all its angles are equal, and know that one or other is sufficient.

As with any model, though, defining levels is at best dubious, but it does help in organising tasks to support the development of understanding of the properties of shapes.

Shape concepts

A teacher is asking the children whether a square is a rectangle and to explain their thinking.

Jane: A square can't be a rectangle because it has four equal sides and a rectangle only has opposite sides equal.

Sam: A square is a rectangle because it has opposite sides equal and four right angles. It doesn't matter that the four sides are equal, it still is a rectangle, just a special one.

Which van Hiele levels would you say Jane and Sam are working at? How would you as teacher develop the discussion so that Jane's concept of square and rectangle are developed?

Toy sort

As a prelude to introducing mathematical shapes, children in a reception class were encouraged to bring their favourite toy to school and asked to describe its shape. The teacher asked whether the shape of their toy looked the same from the back and the front or from one side to the other. She then put all the toys in the middle of the table and asked each child to take two toys and describe the similarities and differences between them. Next she asked them to think about how they could sort all the toys into two piles The children started to sort them under the headings of cars or dolls, hard or soft, big or small, wheels or legs.

Moving on from sorting everyday objects, children may have more abstract shapes to manipulate and describe so that concepts of straightness, curves and sameness can start to emerge. Children can be encouraged to try to roll 3-dimensional shapes down an incline so that the concepts are associated with the properties of the objects. Curved objects will roll, straight ones have sharp ends.

The faces of these mathematical objects will lead to the development of defining 2-dimensional shapes. A cuboid will have squares and rectangles, a pyramid will have triangles, a prism will have triangles and rectangles, and a cylinder will have circles, and so on.

A database can be set up on the computer where all the properties of each object are listed. Shapes can then be sorted to certain criteria and like the activity above can be classified accordingly.

The development of mathematical language associated with shapes is vital and the use of ordinary English words like 'box' instead of 'cuboid' is fine as long as children know they are interchangeable and that 'square boxes' or cubes are also cuboids.

Visualising shapes is an important aspect of conceptual development. Children who always see a square on a page as having one pair of sides vertical and the other horizontal find it difficult to recognise a square 'off-centre' as another square.

All too often shape and space activities are restricted to children naming shapes. Work in shape and space can provide rich opportunities for problem solving activities in the same way that work in number can. In order to structure the design of problems there are four different types of challenges that children might be presented with that involve:

- describing;

- representing;

- constructing;

- classifying.

These are in a rough order of ascending difficulty. The nature of each type of problem context is described below, together with some examples of the sort of challenges and problems that children might tackle.

Describing problems

These are problems and challenges that require children to talk about shapes in a way so that others can identify the shapes and their properties. Often this is done by having a collection of objects on the table and inviting children to talk about the different shapes that they can see. The main drawback with this approach is that everyone else can also see the shapes so the need to be precise in describing is not also present.

A way to encourage children to be more precise is to work with shapes that are hidden from either some or all of the group. The following activities are examples of how this might be done:

Feely bags

Putting shapes in a bag that the children cannot see through and then asking them to describe the shapes. Can the other children identify the shape?

Put each shape from a set of mathematical 3-dimensional shapes into separate cloth bags and give one to a child. Ask this child to feel inside the bag without looking and describe anything they can about that object while the rest of the class have to guess what it is. (Depending on the age and level of attainment of the class you might have a set of all the shapes on the table labelled with their correct names.) Repeat this until all the bags have been identified. Each time a shape is identified correctly take it out of the bag and place it on the table and ask the children to describe anything else they notice about it.

There are several ways in which the basic activity can be varied. For example, children could be given a bag containing a variety of shapes and a matched set of shapes put on the table. The children take it in turns to describe one of the shapes that they can feel inside the bag. The rest of the children have to try and identify which is the matched shape that they can see.

Behind the screen

In this case, one child can see a shape but the rest of the group cannot. This can be set up simply by using a large book to screen off the shape from the rest of the group. Can the child describe the shape, without using its name, so that the rest of the group can identify it?

Representing problems

As adults we move freely between 2-dimensional representations of objects and the actual 3-dimensional objects themselves. For example, asked what the object below is, many people will answer 'cube'.

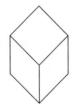

However, this is not a cube, but a representation of a cube. And further, it is a stylised mathematical representation. Cubes do not actually look like that. In the same way that children have to learn to read meaning into the symbols of arithmetic, so too do they need to learn to read meaning into the representation of shape. This is best done through problems that either challenge children to make sense of other people's representations or to make their own. Here are two examples of such challenges.

Buildings

(moving from a 2-dimensional representation to 3 dimensions).
What is the smallest number of cubes required to make a building that looks like this:

FRONT   SIDE

Plans

(moving from 3 dimensions to representing in 2 dimensions.

Take ten interlocking cubes. Make a shape using all the cubes.
Use paper and pencil to represent your shape in some way, so that another person can make it.

Constructing problems

These are problems that build on problems of description and representation but require children not simply to identify shapes on the basis of description but also to use the description as a basis for constructing objects.

In the bag

These are challenges that are similar to feely bag activities. The additional challenge here is that rather than simply identifying the shape in the bag, children have to listen to the description and construct a matched shape. There are several ways in which this might be set up for children to work in pairs or a small group. Each is based on a shape made out of a small number, say eight, of interlocking cubes.

- A shape in a bag is passed around a group. Each person feels it, and describes it to the group. Once they have all described it they each try and build it before it is removed from the bag.

- One child builds an object behind a screen, telling her partner what she is doing. Her partner has to follow the instructions as they go and build an identical shape.

- The shape is in a bag so that neither child can see it. One child puts her hand in the bag and describes the shape to her partner who has to build a replica.

(The most challenging version of this activity is where the child who is building the shape can ask as many questions as she likes of her partner who is feeling the shape but CANNOT start to build the solid until she is sure she can do so without any further information. Once she starts to build, her partner must only watch and cannot provide any further information.)

Under the table

In a group of around four, each person makes the same shape from five cubes. Everyone holds their shape under the table and takes it in turns to add another cube, describing the action so that everyone else can add a cube in the same place. When everyone has had a turn, compare the results. Are the shapes all the same?

Half

This is half a shape.

- What different whole shapes could you make?
- What if it were a quarter of the whole shape?

Fido

Use interlocking cubes to make a small dog.

■ If you made the smallest doorway to fit round Fido, how many cubes wide would it be? How many cubes tall? How many cubes would you need to build the doorway?

■ If you made the smallest kennel for Fido, how many cubes would it need?

■ If you made the smallest carrying case with a lid for Fido, how many cubes would it take?

Classifying problems

These are problems and challenges that require children to begin to look more closely at the mathematical properties of shapes and how the structure of shapes means that some properties are inter-dependent. For example, to construct a four-sided shape with four right-angles means that the opposite pairs of sides have to be parallel to each other. However, the reverse of this structural result is not always the case: it is possible to construct a four-sided shape with opposite pairs of sides parallel which does not have four right-angles.

'Fill the grid' is a particularly effective activity for encouraging children to explore the relationships between properties. In particular, not all of the spaces can be filled. Having to explain why some combinations of properties are impossible can help children begin to develop ideas of proof.

Bungalows

As a group make a collection of bungalows, each made out of five cubes.

■ How many different ways can you sort them?

Fill the grid

■ Can you create four-sided 2-dimensional shapes to fill each cell?

■ Some cells are impossible to fill. Can you explain why?

■ Can you name the shapes?

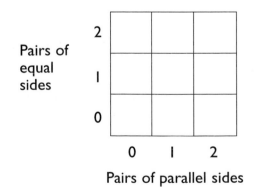

Symmetries

How many different shapes can you make that are symmetrical using these three pieces?

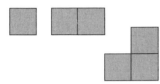

Plain shapes

Kate was following the instructions on a work card. She had a box of plastic shapes, each of which had printed on it the name of the shape. For example the 'squares' had the word square printed on them.

The work card give a list of names of 'plane' shapes and the instruction to find an example of each type of 'plane' shape and draw round it.

Kate had taken the shape named 'triangle' from the box but was hesitating drawing round it. When asked what the problem was she replied 'the shape isn't plain, because it's got the word triangle on it'.

Kate's confusion over the language of plane/plain demonstrates that, although work on shape and space may have a strong practical and visual element, the language side cannot be neglected. All activities need to be accompanied by plenty of discussion about the terminology involved.

Teaching and learning about measures

There are two aspects of learning to measure:

1) **Why we measure:** to find out how much there is of something, to find the extent of something.

2) **How we measure:** by repeatedly using a unit with which to count.

In order to appreciate both of these aspects, there are three key sets of ideas that children need to have experience of and appreciate (in addition to having a good knowledge of number):

- continuity;

- units;

- scales.

Each of these is exemplified below through discussion of one particular measure: area. Similar examples can be found for other measures.

Continuity

Appreciating continuity means knowing about the distinction between **discrete quantities** and **continuous quantities.**

- Discrete quantities are things that can be counted, for example, people, leaves, tables.

- Continuous quantities are things that cannot be counted, for example, a person's height, the weight of a book.

- Measurement is the means by which we can use counting to find out how much.

Before actually starting to measure objects, children need experiences to help them appreciate the continuous nature of properties and of objects. Part of this involves introducing them to the appropriate language – the terms used to begin to recognise the need to measure. With respect to area this would include terms like, covers, edge, surface

Another pre-measuring understanding is comparison – deciding which is the largest, or smallest without measuring. Area-based activities that children might engage in include:

- comparing hands – own two hands, compare with neighbour's hand, fingers spread out, fingers closed. Whose hand is biggest?

- cutting out and ordering in size photographs from newspaper

- comparing leaves.

Units

Appreciating the need for measuring units comes from encountering situations where direct comparison is not possible. If a child wants to know if she is taller than her friend, they only have to stand back to back. But finding out if she is taller than a pen-friend requires some intermediate tool to allow for indirect comparison.

The first stage of indirect comparison is to use a tool that is almost the same size as the objects being compared. To find out if the desk surface is larger or smaller than the notice board, a large sheet of paper could be folded to exactly cover the desk and then transferred to the notice board.

However, it is not always practical to use a single tool to indirectly compare. To find out if the area of one classroom's floor was greater than that of another, covering the entire floor with sheets of taped together paper might do the trick, but not very effectively. Hence the use of a unit that can be repeatedly used to indirectly compare. For example:

- using hands to compare the surface areas of two different tables;

- drawing around two hands and using counters to compare the areas;

- using cubes to compare the areas of pages in two different books.

Through experience of a range of non-standard units, children can come to appreciate that some types of units are more effective than others. So square units are useful for measuring area as they fit together without gaps. Children can then work with standard units.

Scales

Although young children are likely to count units, it is important that when measuring items off against a scale the ratio aspect of comparison is given as much attention as the difference aspect. Knowing that one surface is 2 square metres and another is 6 square metres provides the information that:

- one is 4 square metres bigger than the other, and

- one is three times as big as the other.

This latter, ratio comparison, needs to be emphasised so that later on children can work effectively with ratio and proportion and not fall back on naive strategies that rely on addition (see Chapter 5).

Goldilocks

This is how one teacher chose to use the story of Goldilocks and the Three Bears to provoke data handling activity:

I started by miming the story of Goldilocks and the Three Bears with some Year 2 children. I didn't tell them the story first – they had to guess it. I used an infant chair for the SMALL chair, the table top for the LARGE chair and an adult's chair for JUST RIGHT. In my mime I played Goldilocks coming to the bears' house and finding the door open, I slipped in. I found the three chairs of different sizes. I sat on the small chair and made expressions to show it was too small. I then sat on the table top and dangled my legs to show it was too big and then moved to sit in the adult chair and smiled satisfyingly to show it was just right.

I then asked the class to tell me the story I had acted out as they remembered it. This led to a discussion about what 'just right' might mean. How could we tell if a chair is just right for us? Are the classroom chairs just right for us? What sizes of chairs should we have?

In the discussion that followed I had to give careful instructions on how to sit properly (many don't really know) I asked tall, small and in-between children to sit on a 'demonstration chair'. I also drew stick figures to show sitting, straight-backed with support in the small of the back – these helped show the lower leg length compared to the seat height.

This led to the need to take measurements of our lower legs and of the chairs in the room. We used an unmarked stick for this and I allowed them to choose who measured their knee height in case some were sensitive about being touched by others.

I put a chart up on the bottom of the wall and each child put their knee height on the chart by drawing down the stick from the point they had marked. We did this in order of height and I wrote their names at the bottom of their line. I then marked a horizontal line to show the chair height so that it crossed all the lines on the chart.

We found the middle child's knee height (I said it was the median but didn't dwell on the name) and we agreed this could represent the average height. We then sat down and discussed whether the fact that this height was above the chair height meant the chair was too big or too small and how much difference there needs to be before a chair became too big or too small. We borrowed a chair from the upper end of the school and the children tried that for size. In the end the consensus was to stick with the infant chairs for now.

Children at this age will have had some measurement experience and some may be able to use a ruler. As the task is about comparison of heights it is not necessary to employ any form of standard unit. Using a stick rather than wool or string makes measuring more accurate as some children will stretch the string more than others. In addition the stick does not have a zero marked on it so there is no need for discussion about whether to start measuring from one or zero.

The task the teacher has presented here is rich in opportunities for communication starting from the class having to recount their interpretation of the mimed story. The children have to measure each others' knee heights with the stick and decide on how to mark it and then transfer the mark to the graph in order of size. Deciding on where to put their line can involve the children in much discussion and the teacher can encourage equivalent forms of language like 'bigger than', 'longer than', 'taller than', and so on.

ACTIVITY 1   *Two-piece tangram*

This activity covers several aspects of 2-dimensional shapes from a simple starting point. It requires the children to make, describe and discuss 2-dimensional shapes and to explore the properties of irregular and regular 2-dimensional shapes. In terms of using and applying mathematics children will need to devise suitable methods of representing 2-dimensional shapes, orally and pictorially, and to work co-operatively.

Organisation

You need to prepare materials for a two-piece tangram for each pair of children. These are best made out of thin card and a square 15 cm by 15 cm is a manageable size. You could either prepare the tangrams in advance, storing the two pieces in an envelope, or have the template photocopied onto card so that children can cut out the pieces themselves.

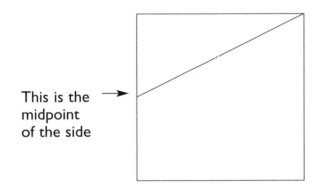

This is the
midpoint
of the side

Starting off

If you have an overhead projector children can come to the front and make shapes that are projected onto the screen. Otherwise you need to start the activity off with the children sitting around in a circle either on the floor or round a table so that they can all see the pieces.

Invite a child to come and fit both pieces together to make a new shape. Discuss the new shape. Get the child to trace a finger around its perimeter to mark out the sides. Work with the children on counting the number of sides the shape has. Can the children name the shape? Invite another child to come and make a different shape.

Developing the activity

Children work in pairs, trying to make shapes with different numbers of sides. In theory, 3, 4, 5, 6 and 7 are all possible. Which ones can they find?

Ask the children to make appropriate recordings of the shapes they have made.

ACTIVITY 1   *Two piece-tangram (Continued)*

Sharing outcomes

Share the shapes made and discuss the naming of them. It is likely that some children do not realise that pentagons and hexagons do not have to be regular shapes. For example, both of these shapes are hexagons:

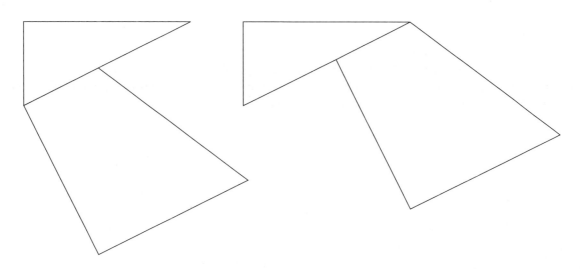

What different sorts of angles can the children find in the shapes?

Talk about the areas of the different shapes made. Do the children realise that the area is always the same?

Questions to ask

- Who can show me a quadrilateral?

- Here is a triangle. Can anyone show me a different way of making a triangle?

Providing for differentiation

All the children should be able to take part in the actual making of the shapes. The activity then allows for some differentiation by outcome as the children are likely to differ in their ability to record the shapes accurately and to put appropriate names to them.

Assessment opportunities

As the children are making and recording the shapes you should be able to observe whether they are being systematic in their searches for new shapes or whether they are simply putting pieces together randomly. Do they make accurate use of tools for recording the shapes?

Communication

The activity requires children to use the language of shape and space accurately to describe the various shapes they make.

ACTIVITY 1 *Two-piece tangram (Continued)*

Progression

Children who succeed well at the task could go on to explore the shapes that can be made with a three-piece tangram.

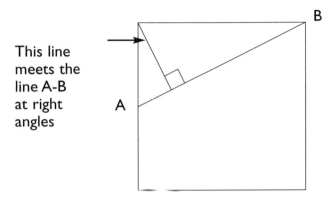

This line meets the line A-B at right angles

Consolidation

Children who need more experience of naming 2-dimensional shapes could create a collage of shapes cut out from magazines and arranged so that shapes with the same number of sides are together. Children could also use strips of card fastened at the ends with brass paper fasteners to make a variety of shapes.

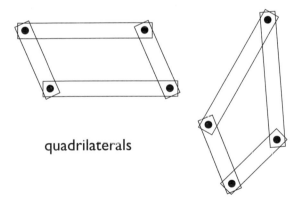

quadrilaterals

Links within the mathematics curriculum

Collections of boxes can be made for children to identify different 2-dimensional shapes that make the faces of the boxes.

Links across the curriculum

The original seven-piece tangram is a puzzle that originated in China. The activity could be linked to a topic on toys and games from around the world.

This activity is adapted from Askew, Ebbutt and Williams (1996).

ACTIVITY 2 *Lost weights*

This activity requires children to use problem solving strategies to solve a practical weighing problem. It also serves to strengthen their knowledge of addition and subtraction of tens to find solutions. In terms of using and applying mathematics, the children will need to reason through methods of solving the problem and devise appropriate ways of recording their findings.

Organisation

Pairs of children will need access to a set of balance scales and two weights: one 250g and one 50g. They will also need a supply of discrete items that are small enough to 'flow' and act like a continuous quantity, for example dried rice or small beans.

You need to prepare 'shopping lists' of the following quantities, either by putting them up on the board or overhead projector, or by duplicating them for the groups.

Shopping list

50g of carrots

300g of bananas

200g of grapes

25g of peas

100g of onions

75g of tomatoes

Starting off

Check that the children know how to use the scales accurately by getting them to balance some items against each other. Remind the children how to use the two available weights by getting one of them to weigh out 50g of rice.

Developing the activity

Ask the children to imagine that the rice (or beans) represents different fruits and vegetables. Direct their attention to the 'shopping list'. Explain that the shopkeeper has lost all of her weights apart from the 250g and 50g weights. Can the children find ways to measure out the different amounts? Encourage the children to experiment to see if they can find more than one way to weigh out each amount and to record their methods.

Sharing outcomes

Discuss with the children their different solutions. Which amounts were the easiest ones to do? Can anyone suggest a different way of getting a certain amount?

Questions to ask

■ What would happen if you put a weight in each of the balance pans?

■ What would happen if you split that amount between the two pans?

■ Are there other amounts that we could measure out just using these two weights?

ACTIVITY 2   *Lost weights (Continued)*

Providing for differentiation

There are a variety of solutions to the problem so there is scope for the activity to provide differentiation through outcome. The choice of weights and amounts to be weighed out could be altered to make the task either more challenging or simpler.

Assessment opportunities

It is likely that the children will use different strategies to solve the problem. For example, 200g could be weighed out by repeatedly weighing out 50g or by putting the 50g into one side of the balance pan and the 250g in the other and adding rice to the 50g side until it balances. Observing the children's approaches and strategies will provide assessment opportunities.

Communication

The need to explain their methods of solution to the other children will encourage clear mathematical talk.

Progression

Challenge the children to select two weights and make up their own problems to swap with another pair.

Consolidation

Children who are finding the problem challenging might benefit from working on a similar challenge, using Plasticine. The children are given a lump of Plasticine weighing 200g. Can they divide the Plasticine up and use the balance pans to create weights of 100g, 50g, 25g, 75g?

Links within the mathematics curriculum

Similar challenges can be provided in other measurement areas. For example, given lengths of ribbon 15cm and 20cm long how could the following lengths be measured out: 10cm, 30cm, 50cm and so on. Given measuring cylinders that hold 100ml and 500ml of liquid how can you measure out 250ml, 400ml, 350ml?

Links across the curriculum

Children could research the history of our system of weights.

ACTIVITY BANK FOR SHAPE, SPACE AND MEASURES

Shape scavenger hunt

Agree on a shape or a number of shapes. In a given amount of time, how many examples of the shape(s) can the children find in the classroom or around the school?

Cuboids

Over time, build up a collection of cuboids from school and those that children bring in from home.

Can the children put them in order of size? How could they check?

What shapes do they get when a cardboard cuboid is cut into its six faces?

Can the children tape the faces back together along some of their edges so that they fold up to form a cuboid again? Are there different ways of doing this?

Kim's game

Put a range of 2-dimensional and 3-dimensional shapes out and allow the children to look at them for a while. Cover them up with a cloth and secretly you (or a child) remove one. Reveal the shapes. Can the children say which one is missing?

Right angles

Fold a piece of paper to make a right angle:

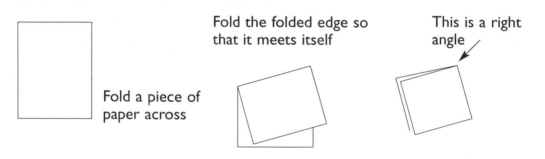

Fold a piece of paper across

Fold the folded edge so that it meets itself

This is a right angle

Use the folded right angle to find angles that are a right angle, greater than a right angle, less than a right angle.

Can the children make a five-sided shape that contains two right angles? Can they make a pentagon that has more than two right angles?

What is the largest number of right angles that a hexagon can have?

Co-ordinates

Choose four different single-digit numbers, for example 2, 3, 7, 8.
Make co-ordinates by taking pairs of these numbers, for example (2, 3) or (8, 8).
Which of the following shapes can the children make by plotting some of these co-ordinates:

■ square, rhombus, kite, rectangle, parallelogram, trapezium, irregular quadrilateral.

ACTIVITY BANK FOR SHAPE, SPACE AND MEASURES (Continued)

Pin drop
How can you find the weight of a single pin?

Bags of weights
In four small plastic bags, make marble weights by sealing into the bags 1, 2, 4 and 8 marbles respectively. Can the children find ways to weigh out the equivalent of every amount from one 'marble's worth' to 15 'marble is worth'?

In a minute
Get the children to make a poster of the number of things they can do in one minute, for example

- throw and catch a ball 20 times;

- count to 120;

- write my name 12 times.

Water consumption

- How many litres of water do the children estimate the school uses for drinks at lunchtime? How could they check?

- How much water does the school use in a day? In a week?

Shoulder to shoulder
If all the children in the school stood shoulder to shoulder, how far would they stretch?

8

HANDLING DATA AND PROBABILITY

Introduction

The bulk of mathematics is concerned with things that can be precisely determined: the sum of 2 + 2, the area of a triangle, the number of diagonals on a polygon. In contrast, much of what happens in our lives cannot be precisely determined: the weather tomorrow, how long I might live, who will win the cup. Probability is the branch of mathematics that examines the indeterminate.

The language of probability is very familiar; words like maybe, chance, possibly, perhaps, all denote the everyday recognition of uncertainty and chance. 'It might rain today', 'There's a good chance he'll be late' are common phrases in use yet the topic carries a great deal of mystique. The national lottery has popularised this branch of mathematics although the lack of understanding of the laws of probability still remain a mystery to most of the population. Despite theoretical evidence people still hold a range of beliefs that defy these laws.

Probability involves the challenge of measuring – things that seemingly can't be measured, things as strange as 'the likelihood of events happening'. So what is it we try to measure and what do we measure this likelihood against?

Consider these statements:

- What's the chance of our train being on time?

- It is always raining when I have to take games or I'm on break duty.

- If it's Wednesday the car won't start.

- I bet Darren won't finish his work before Friday.

- She's always late – Oh! hello, you're early.

- If I rush for the bus, it's bound to be late.

- If I see a bargain it's certain I've not got the money or I've left my cheque book behind.

How quantifiable are these? Does it matter? What makes us say these things and believe them? Is it all about the experiences we have had and the way we intuitively build up a sense of what is likely to happen and what is not?

Our lives are built around the need to be able to make the best decisions based on our experience of the world and what has gone before. In a similar way, mathematicians like to make predictions about future events and have built a theory around uncertainty and randomness – the theory of probability.

Data handling is the branch of mathematics that deals with the tools and instruments for helping people to make sense of a whole range of information. Graphs, charts and numerical data on a whole range of statistics are presented to us daily in the newspapers and on television and radio. The data handling techniques we teach throughout a child's schooling should help them to make sense of these representations and to understand what is really being represented – or misrepresented! Data handling, then, involves collecting, organising, summarising and presenting data in a way that is easy to interpret and communicate.

Probability sits easily with data handling as many activities which help children to understand the notion of chance and randomness involve collecting and analysing large amounts of data. This chapter examines these two important aspects of mathematics: data handling and probability.

National curriculum expectations

At Key Stage 1 there is no separate attainment target for data handling or probability. However in the Programme of Study for number it is specified that children should be able to sort, classify, make comparisons and search for patterns through work on number, shape and space and handling data. It is also expected that children should engage in collecting, recording and interpreting data and represent this data through a range of charts, diagrams, tables and graphs.

At Key Stage 2 handling data has its own Programme of Study. Children are again expected to collect, represent and interpret data, including the use of computers both as a source of data and a means of representing data. They should be able to use and interpret a range of graphical representations, including block graphs, pictograms and line graphs, pie charts.

Key Stage 2 children also need to be introduced to the different sorts of averages: the mode, the median and the mean in relevant contexts, and the range as a measure of spread.

All of these data handling techniques and understandings can be used to help develop work in probability. The Key Stage 2 Programmes of Study require children to work with probability, both through experiment and theory. In the case of the former this involves making estimates of the probability of an event happening or the collection of data and by looking critically at the number of times things occur. For example, repeatedly rolling two dice, collecting together the class's results and counting up the frequency of seven as the total occurring.

Theoretical probability is calculated on the basis of the likelihood of events happening, without actually gathering empirical data. There are 36 possible combinations when two dice are rolled and six of these have a total of seven. So the theoretical probability of a seven being the total rolled is $\frac{6}{36}$ or $\frac{1}{6}$.

They should discuss events and simple experiments and work with vocabulary such as fair, unfair, likely, equally likely and so on. This should lead to children understanding that the probability of any event occurring must be between impossible and certain and expressed as a value between 0 (impossible) and 1 (certain).

Teaching and learning about data handling

Data handling techniques can be applied for a variety of reasons:

1) **Description:** The characteristics of a group can be explored for particular features. A class of children can be described by average height, average age, and so on, and by tabulating the data various graphs and charts can be drawn to show the extent of variations in the group.

2) **Comparison:** Two or more data sets can be explored for similarities and differences.

3) **To find relationships:** What effect does one variable have on another? Is there a causal relationship?

Computer software can remove the drudgery from many data handling activities and can free the child to explore ways of presenting data which communicate the message the child is trying to make in the most effective way. Children can develop their skills of planning, hypothesising and predicting using larger sets of data than could be realistically be handled manually, making trends and emerging patterns easier to observe and predict.

There are five aspects of data handling:

- collect data;
- record data;
- process data;
- represent data;
- interpret data.

PCAI cycle

Alan Graham (1991) suggests that a crucial element is missing here which occurs at the beginning of the data handling process – and that is having a *purpose* for collecting the data. There must be an initial question that prompts the data collection. This in turn will help decide the type of data to be collected and the way in which the data is recorded, processed, represented and interpreted. He suggests four stages in this process which he calls the *PCAI* cycle :

Stage 1	P	Pose the question
Stage 2	C	Collect the data (collecting and recording)
Stage 3	A	Analyse the data (processing and representing)
Stage 4	I	Interpret the results (interpreting)

By encouraging this view of statistics, Graham hopes that children 'might come to see data-handling techniques as genuinely useful skills which can help them to answer questions which they might pose for themselves' and that they might become 'active statistical investigators rather than merely passive handlers of data'.

Sorting and classifying a set of objects

Children can be encouraged to sort a range of different objects, mathematical and natural, in a number of different ways. For example, it is by sorting a pile of buttons by size, by colour and by the number of holes rather than just by one of these classifications that they come to an understanding of sorting having a variety of possibilities.

Collecting, recording and interpreting data

Data collection can be either primary (collected yourself) or secondary (collected elsewhere, for example from a database, newspapers, and so on). Surveys and questionnaires need to be carefully thought out so their purpose is clear. Sample size needs to be considered. Some pre-planning of how the data is to be recorded will be necessary to avoid unnecessary duplication of effort and if too many transfers of the data from one record to another take place then mistakes will start to occur. The level of accuracy is another consideration and the ability of the class to measure to a particular degree of accuracy may affect the data that you want them to collect. For example, asking 7-year-olds to measure their handspans requires measurement skills that may be beyond their capabilities and will make the data unusable since the level of accuracy to make the data useful for later analysis would require the use of millimetres.

Graphs are often used for analysing data. However, the form of the graph needs to be carefully considered to match both the level of children's understanding and their ability to draw graphs. Consideration should be given as to whether a computer package that draws simple graphs – block graphs, pie charts or scattergraphs – might be appropriate for younger children whose drawing skills mean the graphs would take too long or be too difficult to construct, or for older children for whom a comparison of ways of presenting their analysis of the data might be a valuable exercise.

Interpreting tables

Tables and graphs of data without some written analysis can seem meaningless to the reader who has not been involved in the investigation. Children need to interpret their tables and be able to articulate their findings whether through a written summary or a verbal description of their findings.

Measures of average

There is a lot of confusion about the different measure of averages. Mode, mean and median are all a valid measure of average.

The **mode** is the most frequently occurring in a sample and can be identified in a histogram or bar chart.

The **median** is the mid-way value in a data set and if data is presented in ascending or descending order in a bar chart or histogram then the median can also be identified.

The **mean** is the sum of all the values in the set divided by the number of elements in that set. When an average is talked about (as in cricket) it usually refers to the mean.

Drawing conclusions from statistics and graphs

Children need to be taught to be sceptical about the reports they hear or read about which quote statistics like 'three out of four children prefer Big Macs'. They need to be taught to ask questions such as, 'How many children were asked?' 'What did they prefer Big Macs to?', 'In what context was the question being asked?'

Stories provide a context for mathematical activity with which children can engage. In the account below the giant's belt spawned a good deal of mathematical activity based on data handling questions.

The giant's belt

A strange object is found buried deep in the woods, which turns out to be the buckle from a giant's belt. From the size of the buckle, can you tell how big the giant's belt will be?

The teacher used this scenario to discuss averages. The pupils looked at different belts that they were wearing as the teacher posed the questions:

- Would the same belt fit the whole class?

- What would the size of the average belt be?

- How could we find out?

The class got into groups of eight. After much discussion it was decided that each member of the group would produce two paper belts that fitted them. One of these two belts was joined together with the belts of all the other members of the group to make one large belt out of the eight individual ones. This large belt was then equally divided into a number of pieces that would give each member of the group a new belt. This was then the average belt for that group and each child could see how close to the average they were by comparing this with their other belt. Many were surprised that no-one had a belt the same size as the average belt, and that the average belt differed from group to group. Some immediately saw the impact of adding the teacher's belt to their group when he offered to join in and shooed him away.

The PCAI cycle in this activity can be analysed as follows:

P: The problem posed was to find the average size belt for a group of children.

C: The data was collected by making two paper belts for each child and then using one from each child to construct the average belt.

A: The analysis was made by each child comparing the average belt to their own.

I: The interpretation was to see that some children were above average and some were below and that different groups had different average belt sizes indicating the nature of the data set would affect the average, and that including someone like the giant in the group would seriously distort the average belt and be unrepresentative of the sample and therefore an inappropriate means of denoting the average.

This teacher is very committed in his belief that the ideas ought to come from the children. He encourages group discussion to help the children to decide on ways in which they might solve problems and allows them to follow an idea through even if he thinks it might be wrong, as he views this as part of the learning process. He sees this as an assessment opportunity. Asking if he could join his belt to the group is another assessment opportunity he took to see if the children were beginning to develop an understanding of mean.

Other body measurements and relationships can be collected and analysed, the notion of purpose being an important factor. Is the tallest person in the class the fastest runner? If we know the size of the giant's belt and the size of the average class belt, could you work out how tall the giant is? What would be the size of his footprint? Can you make his glasses?

A spreadsheet and database facility would be very useful here as children could each enter the data they think they might need to collect to answer these questions.

Because this is a group activity and practical in nature mixed attainment groups would be quite appropriate as the children would naturally help each other. For those who understand about means the different means for each group could be used to find ways of a calculating a class average and the accuracy of this data investigated.

The class were involved in using and applying their skills of measuring. Dividing up the group belt might have been undertaken differently if there were five or six children in the group. In the latter case the children might have folded the belt into half and then into thirds, an ideal opportunity to bring out some discussion on fractions – a half of a third equals a sixth. However, dividing into five is more problematic. Measuring or trial and improvement might be the only possibilities.

Teaching and learning about probability

Probability can be explored using children's prior experiences.

Teachers' interpretations of pupils' levels of understanding can be made using the following framework:

- What children say – the **intuitions** they bring to a situation.

- What children bring to the situation – their **past experiences** of similar situations.

- What children may do next – the **experiments** that may help to develop their understanding of similar situations.

- How children's perceptions have changed – the **assessment** of the development of their understanding.

The weather

A group of children aged 9 to 11 were asked about what the weather might be like tomorrow and why they thought this.

'I was surprised that the temperature had increased from 1 to 10 in one day, so it might be back to 1 tomorrow.'

'If there was a north wind we would definitely have snow.'

'It will probably be windy, but we might have some sun.'

'A bit of rain dropped on my hand and it was freezing cold, so I thought, I bet it's going to snow.'

'It won't snow because it hasn't been snowing so far, and if it was going to snow it would have snowed already.'

The children were then asked a number of questions based on whether they thought we would have a white Christmas. They were first asked what they thought the weather would be like tomorrow in order to initiate the topic.

Then they were asked to consider how we can find out about the weather, and to justify their predictions using their experiences to weigh up the probabilities.

What can the weather be like and why?

Is it likely to snow, rain or be sunny?

Why do we think that?

What do we base our predictions on?

Is there more of a chance it will be sunny than wet or will it be cloudy?

Can we be certain?

The class then got into groups. Each group were invited to discuss what the possibilities were and to list them in order from most likely to least likely. Each child then had to make their prediction for tomorrow and give a reason why they made it. The way they recorded this was dependent on their level of attainment. For example, some children selected a picture card while others made one of their own. The predictions were grouped to find out which was the most frequent prediction.

Next day the class observed the weather (and discovered it was sunny in the morning and raining in the afternoon), so they repeated the predictions process for the next day but this time included morning and afternoon differences.

- Why was so much of this lesson verbal rather than involving written recording?

- What was the purpose of recording events from most likely to least likely?

Recalling experiences and ordering them in a group helps children to use the language of chance and to get a sense that probability can have a value. Also, the values we assign to particular words can lead to debate about how we use words and how they are understood by others. For example, it *will* rain has a greater value in terms of chance than it *might* rain, but does *could* rain have a greater value than *might* rain? Later on pupils will be introduced to the probability scale from 0 to 1. This is a sound basis from which to progress.

The discussion also highlights whether children can recognise the variety of possibilities and whether they can use their experience to develop their intuition. Also, by encouraging discussion, the effects of others' predictions on our own intuitions can be explored.

Ranking the probabilities of different types of weather indicates how children recognise the likelihood or otherwise of events, and also allows the teacher to see how the children's vocabulary indicates a developing understanding of the likelihood of events occurring.

Links within the mathematics curriculum
Predicting the weather can lead to a great opportunity to use computer data and logging equipment to actually record the weather over a period of time and to see whether any patterns emerge.

Links across the curriculum
Asking the class to consider whether the weather forecasters on TV were better at predicting the weather than they are can lead to opportunities in geography to look at weather information. Similarly, asking children why we can't be sure of the weather can lead to links with the national curriculum for geography.

Extensions
Can we get better at making predictions? Experiments can be developed to see if intuition changes through repeated experiences.

ACTIVITY 1 *Sorting us out*

As a prelude to work on bar charts and pictograms, children can be invited to make human bar charts, but first they can work on the idea of sorting themselves into small groups.

Organisation

Put the class into groups of about eight and ask each group to stand in a line facing the front of the class.

Starting off

■ How quickly can you find the tallest person in your group?

Children will soon sort themselves out into a line with the smallest person at one end and the tallest at the other, and in so doing will be engaged in a lot of comparing of heights.

Now ask them to sort themselves by house number, then shoe size or any other numerical measure they can come up with.

You can make it harder by asking them to add the digits of their telephone numbers or adding their birth day and month (24 December becomes 2 + 4 + 1 + 2 = 9 or 24 + 12 = 36)

Developing the activity

Ask them to come and sit down in a big circle and invite discussion about sorting in non-numerical ways, for example eye colour, favourite TV programmes, games or books. As they have got used to lining up, you can now invite them to go and stand in new groups to represent the non-numerical sorting. Now you will have all the children who like Neighbours in one line, all those who like Blue Peter in another and so on.

■ Which is the biggest group?

■ How much bigger is the Blue Peter group to the Neighbours group?

Challenge the class to devise their own methods of recording and depicting lines of children. One idea is to give each child a multilink cube which they place in a particular column on a chart.

■ Which group has shown the information most clearly?

■ Instead of drawing everybody what could we have done instead?

Children can hold their favourite snacks when they stand in a line. This can lead to the notion of designing representative symbols to be used in pictograms.

■ What labels do we need on our drawings to help someone from another class understand what we have been doing?

Sharing outcomes

Children can then share their interpretations and discuss the relative merits of each set of recordings.

ACTIVITY 1 *Sorting us out (Continued)*

Assessment opportunities

- The children's recording will indicate their level of understanding as will the discussion about the best records.

- They will respond to questions like 'what will happen if...?'

- The level of accuracy of their recording will reveal their ability to count and make a record of their counting and you will be able to see whether they have made the link between the sorting activity and the recording activity.

- Older children can be encouraged to write about the activity and what they have learnt. Younger children can recount the lesson to others.

Consolidation

Once children are clearer about what is involved in sorting they can then start to sort a whole range of objects like buttons, coins, leaves or logiblocks. Let them have the freedom to decide on their own sorts but encourage them to sort in more than one way.

- Who can come up with the most ways of sorting these pieces of fabric?

Buttons will be sorted according to size, colour, or even the number of holes. The database programme *Branch* is ideal for encouraging children to think about **binary sorts.** This is where objects are sorted into two categories by asking a question which gives a yes or no answer. For example, 'is the coin circular?'

The children can then draw bar charts to show the numbers of each type in their sorts.

Progression

A combination of the two activities can introduce some children to sorting by two **attributes.** Once children have organised themselves into groups according to favourite snacks, they might then choose to select someone in that group whose favourite cereal is Corn Flakes. If the selection for the second variable is numerical, they can use the method of sorting within the new group introduced at the beginning of this activity.

In the task above the children are sorting into **exclusive** sets. These activities can lead to the introduction of **Carroll diagrams,** where other possibilities can be discussed.

ACTIVITY 1   *Sorting us out (Continued)*

- Who likes Corn Flakes but not Blue Peter?

- How can we find the tallest person in the class?

- What is the median height of the class?

Links within the mathematics curriculum

Sorting can be done with triangles or rectangles so that properties of different types of each **polygon** can be explored. Questions like 'does it have parallel sides?' 'does it have four right angles?' and so on will help identify the difference between a rhombus and a square.

Links across the curriculum

If the sorts are about food then this can link into some work in science on healthy eating. Sorts on leaves can lead to work on the four seasons.

ACTIVITY 2 *Games of chance*

Many of the games children play are dependent on chance. This activity is designed to develop their awareness of risk and fairness by playing a number of games and then by making up a game that is fair.

Organisation

Have a number of board games around that children like to play and enough so that everyone gets a choice. Children can work in groups of four.

Starting off

- Which games rely on luck?

Children's intuition tells them which games are games of chance and which are games of skill.

- Are the rules fair? Describe a game which is fair or not fair.

Here you can find out about children's intuition and experiences about their chances of winning. (Do they win if they go first?)

A game is fair if you play it properly. (11-year-old)

You might win if you had a better team. (7-year-old)

You'd win at Connect 4 if you were 16 and your opponent was five. (11-year-old)

How can I make a dice come down on six? Just 'please' it. (9-year-old)

Is there an easiest number to get on a dice?... They're all hard if you want them. (8-year-old)

If you throw the dice you might not get it (the number you want). (5-year-old)

Is there a hardest number to get on a dice? A 4 until I'm near the end and I can't get one. (5-year-old)

ACTIVITY 2   *Games of chance (Continued)*

Developing the activity

- Describe a game where you have an even chance of winning.

Ask the class to select a game that they think is fair and play it a few times. Ask them whether it matters who goes first. Did they need one die, two dice, a spinner or a coin?

- Are some numbers easier to get than others?

Many children think that a six or a one are the hardest numbers to get. This discussion can develop their understanding that given a fair die, the chances of any number coming up are equally likely. You might like to group children to debate this topic. Find out how many think it's harder to get a six than a three, for instance, and group them with children who think it is equally likely. Get them to discuss why they each think they are right and then get each group to agree (if possible!). Each group reports back on the consensus. A series of dice-tossing experiments can follow where large samples are collected. Each child can throw a dice 20 times and the total amount of each number thrown collected and recorded on the board.

Assessment opportunities

Identify some of the games you have played a lot which involve a die. Tell someone how to play the game to win.

This will help you find out what intuitions they have developed about how the die influences the game.

Can you change the game to improve your chances of winning? Will it also improve their opponent's chances?

This will test the new intuitions and identify understanding of what is more likely.

Extensions

If you use a die, what possibilities are there?

This question can lead to some theoretical work on probability for those children who might find this interesting and are able to cope with the arithmetic.

Are there different ways of winning?

Consolidation

Children can be invited to devise their own games that they consider to be fair. They can invite others to play it and be the judge of the fairness of the game.

ACTIVITY BANK FOR DATA HANDLING

Travel

Gathering data on the different modes of transport that the children use to travel to school is a popular activity, but it is important to use the data for a purpose and make predictions from it. Questions you might ask the children include:

■ If we did this again tomorrow, would the graph look the same?

■ If we asked another class in the school for the same information, how likely is the graph to be similar?

■ If we asked children in (name of a nearby school or place) how similar do you think their graph would be?

Bird table

Setting up a bird table near the classroom can provide the opportunity for several strands of data to be gathered. Discuss with the children what they think the birds will like to eat. How could they find out the most popular food? How many birds visit the bird table each morning? How many different types of birds visit the table? Is the table more popular at some times of the day than others? Get groups to work on one of these questions and to plan and carry out different ways of collecting and presenting the data.

Best buy

Take into class a selection of packets of different brands of crisps. Which do the children prefer? What are the things that are important in a crisp? Brainstorm the various ideas, which might include things like crispiness, flavour, size, quantity in a packet. Set the children off in groups to discuss how they would find out which of the various brands was the 'best buy'. (Younger pupils could simply work on finding out which was the most popular amongst the class.) Get the children to present their plans for finding out to the rest of the class and encourage the others to offer constructive criticism. Children can have access to the crisps only when you are convinced that their plans are well thought through!

A variation on this activity would be to look at best buys in comics or newspapers.

Planning an event

Planning and then organising an event for the class can provide plenty of opportunity to gather and process data for a purpose. Examples of the sorts of things children could work on include a Friday afternoon picnic, a end of term class sports afternoon or disco, a class cake sale, a trip to the local park and so on. Work with the class on breaking the problem up into various components. For example, an end of term disco might include food, music, games, drink. Different groups can work on different areas gathering and processing data to help them make decisions. So the food group might gather data on how much people were prepared to pay, what food preferences there were and go on to make decisions about how much to charge and what they would provide.

ACTIVITY BANK FOR DATA HANDLING (Continued)

Break your record

Children select a physical skill they would like to challenge themselves on. This might be skipping with a rope, bouncing a ball, hopping on one foot as far as they could or seeing how far they could run in 40 seconds. Select skills that are easy to organise and do not require you to book the hall or gym. Also consider the time of year as running may be problematic in January! Set aside times each day for the children to practise their skill and then to time or record their trials. Decide on how many trials you will allow them to record in one day. Encourage them to work in pairs so that they can record the results for each other. Decide on a fixed time scale for the activity, say three days or a week. Older children can work out their range of scores, while younger children can keep track of their highest and lowest scores each day. Children can record their data in a number of ways; individually or as a group. They can choose whether to record their daily average (and therefore which measure of average they will uses, their individual performance, their estimated performance compared to their actual performance, for example.

ACTIVITY BANK FOR PROBABILITY

Event washing line

String up a washing line across the class and peg at opposite ends labels saying 'certain' and 'impossible'. Prepare in advance some statements on the likelihood of each. Examples might be 'tomorrow morning I will wake up and be the Prime Minister'; 'I will do maths tomorrow'; 'Today is Wednesday, tomorrow will be Thursday'; 'It will rain here this week'; 'It will rain somewhere in the world this week'. Discuss these statements with the children and agree where to peg them on the line. Set the children off in groups to create similar statements to add to the line. Work with the class on writing labels to describe the likelihood of the events happening. For example, 'very, very unlikely' or 'almost certainly'. More experienced children could go on to add probability values between 0 and 1.

Cover up

Show the class or a group of children a bag containing ten coloured cubes or counters in three different colours, for example, five red, three blue, two yellow. Give each child a piece of paper with a grid of six squares on it.

Ask them to treat this as a bingo board – you will draw a cube from the bag and if that colour is on the board the player can cover it up. Make it clear that the cube will go back in the bag each time. Can the children colour in their board in a way that will make it likely that they will win? Once they have coloured the board, play the game. Discuss with the children how they decided on the colourings. The children could go on to make up their own bags of cubes and game boards, perhaps designing some that would make it very unlikely to win on.

Cubes in the bag

Put a collection of around ten coloured cubes or counters in an opaque bag. Have different numbers of each colour, for example, five red, two blue, two yellow, one white. Shake the bag, draw out one cube and note the colour on the board. What can the children say about the colours of cubes in the bag?

Replace the cube and draw out another. What can the children now say about the colours of cubes? Get the children to discuss, in groups, how many times they think you would need to draw and replace a cube before they were confident that they had a good idea of how many of each colour is in the bag. As a whole class discuss their various ideas. Without taking all the cubes out of the bag would it ever be possible to know for certain how many there were of each colour?

Butter side down

People say that when you drop a piece of toast, it always lands butter side down. How true do the children think this is? Can they set up an experiment to find out? (I recommend having available cardboard toast and, say, Plasticine, rather than the real thing!)

Escape

Children will each need a strip of squared paper one square wide and twelve squares long, the squares numbered 1 to 12. They also need six counters each (the squares on the paper need to be large enough for the counters to fit in). Each pair of children needs a pair of 1 – 6 dice. Explain that the squares represent prison cells and the counters are the prisoners. They are going to take it in turn to roll the two dice, find the total and if there is a prisoner in that numbered cell then they can go free. The winner is the player to have all their prisoners released first. Which cells are the children going to place their prisoners in to maximise the chance of them being released? A cell can have more than one prisoner in it, but only one is released at a time. After the children have played the game several times discuss how they decided where to place the prisoners. They could go on to draw up a six by six chart to show all the possible combinations of the two dice and calculate the different probabilities for various totals.

9

USING AND APPLYING MATHEMATICS

Introduction

You may be wondering why I have left 'using and applying mathematics' to the end of this book rather than it appearing at the beginning. The reason for this is that I believe the intentions behind the 'using and applying mathematics' aspects of the National Curriculum have been included implicitly in the previous chapters.

My intention in this chapter is to make more explicit some of the features of using and applying that I think are most important and highlight some of the teaching strategies that might help develop this aspect of the curriculum. The suggestions given here arose from research into the National Curriculum with a group of teachers who were identified as being particularly effective in implementing using and applying mathematics (Askew *et al.* 1993).

What the National Curriculum expects

Although the terms 'using and applying mathematics' imply that this part of the curriculum is mainly to do with the application of mathematics that has been previously learnt, the detail of the National Curriculum presents a different impression of the importance of this part of the curriculum.

First, 'using and applying' indicates that there is a need for pupils to experience a breadth of mathematical contexts through:

- **practical tasks** (for example, designing a board game or constructing a container to hold 500g of rice);
- **real-life problems** (for example, planning an end of the week picnic or deciding on the best layout of chairs for the school concert);
- **investigating within mathematics itself** (for example, investigating what happens when you add two odd numbers together or devising a quick method for being able to calculate 15 per cent of quantities).

In addition to requiring teachers to pay attention to the range of mathematical contexts, using and applying mathematics also means making sure that children are developing their mathematical thinking. The National Curriculum suggests that there are three ways in which this can be encouraged.

Making and monitoring decisions

These mean problem-solving situations that require children to make decisions about the mathematics to use and to check that the decisions they make are sensible ones. For example, in deciding how many egg boxes (holding six eggs) are required to hold 40 eggs, deciding that division is an appropriate operation and that 7 is a more sensible answer than 6 or 4.

Mathematical communication

Being able to talk about mathematics, listen to and understand others, present results for themselves and others and read mathematics are all important aspects of mathematical communication that must be attended to. For example, being able to explain a method for adding two three-digit numbers together and being able to follow someone else's explanation and check that it works.

Reasoning logic and proof

Being able to make simple generalisations, hypotheses and argue through results. For example, being able to generalise that adding any two odd numbers together always gives an even answer and being able to explain why, using diagrams, words or symbols.

Teaching and learning using and applying mathematics

Making and monitoring decisions

Many children's experience of learning mathematics is as a set of rules and procedures. The text book or teacher sets out the method from which the children are expected to learn uncritically. Mathematics is something that is 'transmitted' from the teacher (or text book) to the children. When it comes to applying the method, the amount of decision-making that the children have to make is usually very limited, as we saw in Chapter 6.

Alternatively, children may simply be given a problem to solve and be left on their own to try and find a method of solution. Mathematics is something that children have to 'discover' for themselves.

If we really want children to be able to apply their mathematics then I suggest both the 'transmission' and 'discovery' models have in their most extreme form real limitations. Too heavy an emphasis on 'transmission' can lead to children not thinking about the mathematics for themselves and relying too much on the teacher to tell them what to do. Given a simple problem to solve, the children come and ask, 'is this an add, Miss?'

On the other hand, too much emphasis on children discovering methods for themselves can lead to them using inefficient and inappropriate techniques.

What is required is a style of teaching that falls between these two extremes. One that encourages the children to display some independence in their mathematical thinking but also acknowledges that the teacher plays a key role in helping the children to become more mathematically sophisticated.

Some of the elements of such a style of teaching might include:

- spending time helping children understand a problem;

- building upon pupils' methods, acting as a 'critical friend',

- adopting a questioning, listening and observing style of interacting.

Spending time helping children understand a problem

Understanding a problem and deciding how to try and solve it are closely bound together. The time spent on helping children understand a problem rather than immediately working on strategies for solving pays off in terms of children finding their own strategies and solutions.

As part of the mathematics workshop mornings with her Year 1 class, the teacher always had one or two problems which were identified as being ones that the children could work on independently. One such problem was challenging the children to devise some way of keeping track of how many pieces each jigsaw should have as a means of making sure none were missing. The teacher spent time at the beginning of the lesson discussing with the groups working independently exactly what it was they were to work on. The children knew that they were then expected to work on their own and only seek help from the teacher if they really could not continue. But they also knew that the teacher would spend time with them at the end of the session discussing their solutions.

Building upon pupils' methods

Once children have found a way to tackle a problem it is best to not always leave them to do so in whatever fashion they want. The teacher plays a key role in helping the children develop and extend ideas. One particular strategy which is helpful is to **act as a critical friend:** challenging the pupils by gently provoking them to think about what is going on.

One teacher decided to do some work on index notation with her Year 6 class. The pupils were engaged in a topic on Egypt and she began the mathematics lesson with groups writing 'As I was going to St Ives, I met a man with 7 wives and every wife had 7 cats' and so on using problems with an Egyptian flavour. After the class had shared and enjoyed the different versions of the problem, the teacher worked with them on drawing out and making explicit the underlying mathematical similarities in terms of repeated multiplication. The class discussed various ways that they could use to record the products, the teacher challenging them to use as few terms as possible. Drawing on the strengths and weaknesses of the suggestions the teacher introduced the standard index notation. The lesson finished with the children posing problems for each other that could be recorded in a similar fashion.

Adopting a questioning, observing and listening style of interacting

Acting as a 'critical friend' involves spending time listening to and observing children. It is important to question the children about their responses, both correct and incorrect, and to observe actions closely to help decide what children might be thinking. Although listening may seem like an obvious skill, listening carefully to the reasons that children provide is considerably more difficult than simply listening out for responses which fit with what you as the teacher already know to be correct.

A low-attaining group of Year 3 pupils were working on trying to find the totals of 1 + 2, 1 + 2 + 3 and so on, up to the total of 1 to 10. They managed to answer the first question but seemed to have no idea how to proceed from there. When the teacher joined them they had got no further than writing down 1 + 2 = 3. They could explain how they had worked the first one out but when asked what 1 + 2 + 3 came to, the children seemed only to guess. The teacher directed their attention to 1 + 2 and underlined this in the next string: 1 + 2 + 3. Focusing their attention in this way helped the group arrive at the answer. Adopting a similar approach for 1 + 2 + 3 + 4, everyone agreed the answer would be 10. Excitedly, Lee started bouncing up and down saying that it was going to be 10 add 5 for 1 + 2 + 3 + 4 + 5. The teacher asked him how he was going to work this out.

Lee: You put ten in your brain and five on your fingers and you count 1 2 3 4 5 6 7 8 9 10 in your head and then 1 2, no, 10 11 12 13 14 15 on your fingers.

Later the teacher came back to the group. Lee was so pleased with his method that he had gone beyond the task given and was about to find the total of 1 to 13. Unfortunately he had made a slip up at 8 and his answers from that point were one short. The teacher asked him to talk her through 1 to 13 as he was doing it.

Lee: You put 77 [his answer to 1 to 12] in your head and put out three fingers.

In fact he proceeded to count on from 77 by putting all ten fingers out and pointing to an additional three 'spots' on the table.

Mathematical communication

Mathematical communication takes many forms. What most readily comes to mind are the written forms of communication: answers to calculations, jottings used to help in working things out, graphs from data handling. In addition to written communication, the importance of discussion has been highlighted throughout this book. Ways of increasing the quality and quantity of discussion include:

- engaging in teacher/pupil discussion;

- encouraging pupil/pupil discussion;

- creating an atmosphere where the children feel 'safe' to offer their ideas.

Engaging in teacher/pupil discussion

Children bring a variety of meanings and understandings to discussions and talking with them about mathematics can involve ambiguity. Rather than simply needing correction, the fact that children may not immediately interpret things in the way you do can provide a powerful learning experience. Misunderstandings are not something that get in the way of teaching but a rich source of points of discussion.

Encouraging discussion between pupils

Throughout this book there have been examples of how to set up tasks in ways that both encourage children to talk with each other about the mathematics and provide you with the opportunity to listen, make assessments and support children's explanations if necessary.

A teacher spent time with four Year 6 pupils in establishing the ground rules for a version of 'connect four'. Each had to take it in turns to cover a number on a 1–100 grid by combining the numbers on five playing cards dealt to them (picture cards removed from the pack). Before a number could be claimed, everyone in the group had to agree that it had been correctly calculated.

P1: *Ten, add five, take away five, add nine, take away four is fifteen.*

P2: *Three, add five, eight, add two, ten, times seven, seventy add ten is eighty.*

P3: *Ten, sixteen, add ten, twenty-six, twenty-seven, twenty-eight.*

P4: *Ten add ten is twenty, take away five.*

Teacher: *Subtract.*

P4: *Subtract five is fifteen, add three eighteen, add four twenty-two.*

The teacher drew the children's attention to the way that one of them had successfully blocked someone else and discussed the strategy.

Creating an atmosphere where the children feel 'safe' to offer their ideas

It is important to accept children's solutions and explanations even if these are not totally correct. Rather than setting yourself up as the judge of what counts as right or wrong, encourage the children to decide for themselves.

In the next round of the multiplication game, Momtaz was wanting to get 16, 25, 27 or 36. She could see that she could get 25 with three of her cards and finished with 'six subtract ten is nothing'.

Teacher: Is it nothing?
Poppy: It goes back to minus four.

The teacher discussed with the group which interpretation they should use. Two of the group both argued for the inclusion of negative numbers but the other two were less sure in their understanding of these so they agreed not to work with negative numbers.

Reasoning, logic and proof

Ways in which teachers can help children engage with reasoning, logic and proof include:

- encouraging the search for patterns and generalisations;

- challenging pupils;

- using practical work to provoke mental activity.

Encouraging the search for patterns and generalisations

Encouraging children to seek out underlying patterns or generalisations in their work needs to be a regular and ongoing part of all mathematics lessons. It is helpful to ask the children 'what would happen if ...?' to encourage them to think beyond the particular examples that they are working on.

Challenging pupils

Too often children are given tasks to do in mathematics that they can already do easily. While it is important for children to practise basic skills, this needs to be balanced against posing problems that children might initially find difficult. Rather than always offering 'safe' tasks based on children's firm understandings, challenge them to use mathematics at the edges of their understanding.

A teacher was working with a group of her Year 1 children on developing their sense of tens and ones. She devised a simple game whereby she placed a number of tens and ones blocks under a cloth. Telling the children that she was only going to show them how many there were for a short while and that they would not have long enough to count how many there were, she uncovered the blocks for a few seconds. The children became very involved in the game but despite Jo's instructions they persisted in trying to count the blocks. They all talked about the numbers they had estimated and the teacher explained to them what she did in order to make an estimate, demonstrating by getting the pupils to hide some blocks for her.

Using practical work to provoke mental activity

As stressed throughout this book it is important to encourage children to become involved mentally with the mathematics rather than simply carrying out a practical task.

A teacher was working with a group of four Year 1 children using plastic 1–100 grids designed to hold interlocking cubes. The grids had a reversible inlay numbered 1–100 or 0–99. The teacher deliberately gave one version to two children and one to the other pair. As they were filling the grid with cubes, Mina decided to count her squares and got to 100. She glanced across at Jed's grid and, confused that his finished at 99, kept looking back and forth between her grid and his. Soon she went to get the teacher and brought her over to ask why they were different. The teacher put both grids side by side and they talked about the different numberings.

Difficulties children might have in using and applying mathematics

If children are given problems to solve, whether practical, mathematical or real-life, there will be times when children become stuck, make slow progress or might otherwise benefit from 'expert' advice. There was a time when it was popularly believed that children should be left to find their own way out of such difficulties. I suggest, however, that children need to be taught strategies that will help them make progress.

There are three ways in which you might do this:

- anticipate useful strategies;
- 'model' strategies;
- encourage pupils to share methods.

Anticipating useful strategies

When planning activities for using and applying mathematics it is helpful to have thought through possible helpful strategies so that if the children do not come up with a method for themselves then you know what to suggest.

Chocolate boxes

A Year 6 class were investigating how many ways there are to select three chocolates from a box containing eight different fillings. The children were using diagrams and drawings to generate all the possibilities. The teacher used the opportunity to draw the children's attention to more efficient strategies, using a coding system to avoid repetitive drawings and encouraging the children to abstract the essential mathematics from the investigation, rather than paying too much attention to the context of boxes of chocolates.

'Modelling' strategies

A subtle difference lies between supporting children's own methods and over-directing an activity so that they merely follow someone else's procedure. I suggest that ideas need to be offered more in the spirit of 'here is how I might do it' rather than 'here is how you must do it'.

'Identikit'

A teacher of a Year 3 class set up an activity to focus on being systematic. The children were given a set of 'identikit' features – eyes, ears, noses and mouths – and challenged to find out how many different faces were possible. After the children had been working for a while, their teacher noticed that they were randomly generating the faces. She gathered them together and discussed how they could make sure they had found them all. Once the children seemed to appreciate that being systematic would help, the teacher showed them one possible way of doing this.

The teacher asked the children to start again but this time to make sure they were using a system of some sort, and the teacher challenged them to try and find one different from hers. Most of the children succeeded in doing this and at the end of the lesson they eagerly joined in discussing their different systems.

Encouraging pupils to share methods

As I have indicated throughout this book, getting children to explain to each other how they approached activities is a good way of helping individual children appreciate that there are varieties of methods.

Managing using and applying mathematics

To put the above ideas into practice means organising classrooms and lessons to maximise time for engaging with children on mathematics and minimise teacher time spent on managing the work. Strategies teachers use to do this include:

■ organising classes for pupil responsibility;

■ organising time to work with the whole class, groups and individuals;

■ focusing on a limited number of mathematical activities within lessons.

Organising classes for pupil responsibility

To reduce the time you have to spend on managing the class set things up so that children can take responsibility for ongoing classroom housekeeping. Materials need to be clearly stored and children know that they have free access to any equipment they need.

There are also strategies the teacher can use to reduce the time that children are not engaged with the mathematics.

Working with groups of Year 3 pupils one teacher would frequently stop and ask who understood. The children indicating understanding were given the option of moving off and starting work on the activity. Those still not sure were invited to stay for further discussion. After some weeks of working in this way the pupils knew they could say to their teacher 'I understand' and move away without having to wait to be invited to.

On A4 sheets, the teacher wrote down in simple terms the 'problem' each group was to work on and read these out to the whole class. Her Year 1 children did not always take in what was expected of them at this stage so they were encouraged to use the written instructions and the materials put out for them to try and work out what they had to do. The teacher reinforced this when she joined the group by asking the children to explain to her what they thought they had to do.

Organising time to work with the whole class, groups and individuals

Effective teachers display flexibility in organising their classes. Groupings need to be determined by the nature of the work to be embarked upon rather than through some rigid or routine ways of organising the class. In all the classrooms there should be time for working as a class, in groups and individually (or in pairs).

A Year 1 teacher started her workshop mornings with a whole class mathematical story, game or activity. She supported this with simple 'props' or by involving the children. 'Ten loopy caterpillars' used a set of numeral cards turned over to record the number of caterpillars left. At the end of the workshops at least one group had to report back and the other children then asked them questions about the work. The teacher was firm on this; anyone offering a statement rather than a question was reminded of the rules and she would work with them on either turning their statement into a question or devising some other question.

A Year 3 teacher frequently held whole class discussions on mathematics. Children would share methods they used to work things out or report back. These discussions took place as part of a morning given over to mathematics workshops – usually these were organised around a common theme, with different levels of activity to suit different abilities. Because everyone had been working on similar areas of mathematics involvement the discussion was high and the quality of interchange good.

Effective teachers may employ a variety of organisational styles to work with children to engage their interest, but a common practice is to spend time with the whole class or group discussing the work when introducing new activities. Time spent in this way seems to be a good investment as:

■ children are able to sustain working on the activity;

■ good levels of concentration are brought about;

■ teachers spend less time repeating themselves and are freed to work with children on the mathematics.

Appreciating that time is better spent talking with the children about the activity within the lesson rather than spending time outside the lesson trying to produce 'child proof' workcards means planning time can be used to think about the form and structure of the lesson, rather than preparing resources. You may have noticed that the activities presented in this book do not, on the whole, require extensive preparation in terms of props or other resources.

In working with groups, many teachers employ a variety of strategies not only to make time for this, but also to ensure that every group got a fair share of attention.

A Year 2 teacher had mathematics going on at a variety of times during the day but for the hour before lunch she organised five group activities. At least one of these was a mathematics practice activity and two were language tasks which did not change over the course of the week, so that the children came to a clear understanding of what was expected of them. The fourth group also had independent work to do. This left the teacher free to focus on maths with the fifth group so over the course of the week everyone received some sustained teaching.

A Year 6 teacher planned on a fortnightly basis when she was going to be working with particular groups of pupils.

Teachers also need to create time to work with individuals.

One teacher kept note of who needed help but did not always deal with it immediately. She waited until everyone was settled into their tasks and then sat quietly with individuals. Children knew that during this time they might seek help but were not to disturb the teacher. She kept a selection of games and puzzles in a box by her chair so that children could work on these while waiting for her to be free.

Focusing on a limited number of mathematical activities within lessons

Quality mathematical discussions are demanding to sustain. Organising lessons around a limited range of activities can reduce organisational demands and free up time for discussion. Sometimes children will be engaged in similar tasks, but linked around a common theme. This benefits of this are that:

- the teacher does not have to process as much different information as in a lesson with wide range of activities;

- children have more opportunity to both learn from each other and to be motivated by what other children have done.

One teacher was particularly pleased with the outcome of a morning given over to a set of linked activities all based around the properties of multiples of nine. When the children reported back on what they had done, the lower attainers realised how much more children who had committed their nines times table to memory had gained from the activity. On their comment sheets that the children were given to complete (asking them what they had learnt, what they had difficulty with and what they were going to do next) several of these children committed themselves to learning their tables.

If this book encourages more children to take this attitude of having some control over their learning of mathematics, then it will have served its purpose.

BIBLIOGRAPHY

Anghileri, J. and Johnson, D. C. (1992) 'Arithmetic operations on whole numbers: multiplication and division', in T. R. Post (ed.) *Teaching Mathematics in Grades K-8* (Second edition) Boston, USA: Allyn and Bacon.

Anghileri, J. (1995) 'Division and the role of language in the development of solution strategies', in *Proceedings of the Third British Congress of Mathematics Education,* One (pp. 113 – 120). Manchester Business School, UK, 13 to 16 July, 1995.

Ashlock, R. B. (1982) *Error Patterns in Computation: A semi programmed approach* (third ed.). Columbus, USA: Merrill.

Askew, M., Bibby, T. and Brown, M. (1997) *Raising Attainment in Numeracy: Final Report.* London: King's College, University of London.

Askew, M., Briscoe, R., Ebbutt, S., Maple, L. and Mosely, F. (1995) *Number at Key Stage 1: Core materials for teaching and assessing number and algebra.* London, UK: BEAM/King's College/Tower Hamlets.

Askew, M., Briscoe, R., Ebbutt, S., Maple, L. and Mosely, F. (1996) *Number at Key Stage 2: Core materials for teaching and assessing number and algebra.* London, UK: BEAM/King's College/Tower Hamlets.

Askew, M., Ebbutt, S. and Williams, H. (1996) *Using and Applying Mathematics for 5-7 Year-Olds.* London: Heinemann.

Askew, M. and Ebbutt, S. (1997) *Using and Applying Mathematics for 7-11 Year-Olds.* London: Heinemann

Askew, M., Brown, M., Johnson, D. C., Millet, A., Prestage, S. and Walsh, A. (1993) *Evaluation of the Implementation of National Curriculum Mathematics at Key Stages 1, 2 and 3. Volume 1: Report, Volume 2: Appendix.* London: School Curriculum and Assessment Authority.

Askew, M., Brown, M., Rhodes, V., Wiliam, D. and Johnson, D. (1997) *Effective Teachers of Numeracy: Report of a study carried out for the Teacher Training Agency.* London: King's College, University of London.

Assessment of Performance Unit (1991) *APU Mathematics Monitoring (phase 2).* London: School Examination and Assessment Council.

Basic Skills Agency (1997) *International Numeracy Survey: a comparison of the basic skills numeracy of adults 16 – 60 in seven countries.* London: The Basic Skills Agency.

Baroody, A. J. (1993) *Problem-Solving, Reasoning and Communicating, K-8.* New York: Macmillan.

Beishuizen, M. (1995) 'New research into mental arithmetic strategies with two-digit numbers up to 100', in *European Conference on Educational Research,* University of Bath, September 1995.

Brown, J. S. and Burton, R. R. (1978) 'Diagnostic models for procedural bugs in basic mathematical skills.' *Cognitive Science,* **2**, 155 – 192.

Brown, L., Hewitt, D. and Tahta, D. (eds.) (1989) *Selected Articles by Caleb Gattegno,* reprinted from 'Mathematics Teaching'. Derby: Association of Teachers of Mathematics.

Denvir, B. (1984) *The Development of Number Concepts in Low Attainers in Mathematics Aged Seven to Nine Years.* London: Chelsea College, University of London. Unpublished PhD thesis.

Dickson, L., Brown, M. and Gibson, O. (eds.) (1984) *Children Learning Mathematics: A Teacher's Guide to Recent Research.* Eastbourne: Holt, Rinehart and Winston, for the Schools Council.

Fielker, D. (1978) Editorial. *Mathematics Teaching,* **84,** 2 – 6.

Foxman, D., Ruddock, G., McCallum, I. and Schagen, I. (1991) *APU Mathematics Monitoring (Phase 2).* Unpublished report prepared for Schools Examination and Assessment Council. London: School Examination and Assessment Council.

Fuson, K. (1992) 'Research on whole number addition and subtraction', in D. A. Grouws (ed.) *Handbook of Research on Mathematics Teaching and Learning* (pp. 243 – 275). New York, NY: Macmillan.

Gelman, R. and Gallistel, R. G. C. (1986) *The Child's Understanding of Number.* Cambridge, Mass.: Harvard University Press.

Graham, A. (1991) 'Where is the 'P' in statistics?', in D. Pimm and E. Love (eds.) *Teaching and Learning School Mathematics.* London: Hodder and Stoughton.

Gray, E. M. (1991) 'An analysis of diverging approaches to simple arithmetic: preference and its consequences', *Educational Studies in Mathematics,* **22**(6), 551 – 574.

Hart, K. (ed.) (1981) *Children's Understanding of Mathematics: 11 – 16.* London: John Murray.

Hart, K., Johnson, D. C., Brown, M., Dickson, L. and Clarkson, R. (1989) *Children's Mathematical Frameworks 8 – 13: A Study of Classroom Teaching.* Windsor: NFER-Nelson.

Hughes, M. (1986) *Children and Number: Difficulties in Learning Mathematics.* Oxford: Basil Blackwell.

Lave, J. (1992). 'Word problems: a microcosm of theories of learning', in P. Light and G. Butterworth (eds.) *Context and Cognition.* Hemel Hempstead, UK: Harvester Wheatsheaf.

Markovits, Z. and Sowder, J. (1988) 'Mental computation and number sense', in M. J. Behr, C. B. Lacampagne and M. M. Wheeler (eds.), *Proceedings of the tenth annual meeting of the North American chapter of the International Group for the psychology of mathematics education* (pp. 58 – 64). De Kalb, IL: Northern Illinois University.

McIntosh, A. (1978) 'Some subtractions: what do you think you are doing?' *Mathmatics Teaching*, **83,** 17 – 19.

McIntosh, A., Reys, B. J. and Reys, R. E. (1992) 'A proposed framework for examining basic number sense', *For the Learning of Mathematics,* **12**(3), 2 – 8.

Munn, P. (1994) 'The early development of literacy and numeracy skills'. *European Early Childhood Education Research Journal,* **2**(1), 5 – 18.

Novak, J. D. and Gowin, D. B. (1984) *Learning How to Learn.* New York, NY: Cambridge University Press.

Plunkett, S. (1979). 'Decomposition and all that rot', *Mathematics in School,* **8**(3), 2 – 7.

Robitaille, D. and Dirks, M. (1982) 'Models for the mathematics curriculum', *For the Learning of Mathematics,* **2**(3), 3 – 21.

Ronshausen, N. (1978) 'Introducing place value'. *Arithmetic Teacher,* **25**(4)

Shuard, H., Walsh, A., Goodwin, J. and Worcester, V. (1991) *Calculators, Children and Mathematics.* London: Simon and Schuster (for NCC).

Steffe, L. P. (1983) 'Children's algorithms as schemes', *Educational Studies in Mathematics,* **14,** 109 – 125.

Stigler, J. W., Lee, S. Y. and Stevenson, H. W. (1990) *The Mathematical Knowledge of Japanese, Chinese and American Elementary Schoolchildren.* Reston, V.A.: National Council of Teachers of Mathematics.

Swan, M. (1990) 'Becoming numerate: developing conceptual structures' in S. Willis (ed.) *Being Numerate: What counts?* (pp. 44 – 71). Victoria, Australia: Australian Council for Educational Research.

Thompson, A. G., Philipp, R. A., Thompson, P. W. and Boyd, B. A. (1994) 'Calculational and conceptual orientations in teaching mathematics', in D. B. Aichele and A. F. Coxford (eds.) *Professional Development for Teachers of Mathematics (1994 Yearbook).* Reston VA.: The National Council of Teachers of Mathematics, Inc.

Walkerdine, V. (1988) *The Mastery of Reason: Cognitive Development and the Production of Rationality.* London: Routledge.

Wearne, D. and Hiebert, J. (1988) 'Constructing and using meaning for mathematical symbols: the case of decimal fractions', in J. Hiebert and M. Behr (eds.) *Number Concepts and Operations in the Middle Grades* (pp. 220 – 236). Reston, VA.: Lawrence Erlbaum Associates for National Council of Teachers of Mathematics.

INDEX